MATT DEAN PETTIT

THE GREAT SHELLFISH COOKBOOK

FROM SEA TO TABLE

More than 100 Recipes to Cook at Home

appetite
by RANDOM HOUSE

Appetite by Random House® and colophon are registered trademarks of Penguin Random House LLC.

Library and Archives of Canada Cataloguing in Publication is available upon request.

ISBN: 9780147530578
eBook ISBN: 9780147530585

Food photography and styling by Ksenija Hotic
Illustrations by Donald Pettit
Photo on page i © ayzek/Shutterstock.com;
photo on page 59 © Foxys Forest Manufacture/Shutterstock.com;
photo on page 195 © Adriana Nikolova/Shutterstock.com
Cover and book design by Terri Nimmo

Printed and bound in China

Published in Canada by Appetite by Random House®,
a division of Penguin Random House LLC.

www.penguinrandomhouse.ca

10 9 8 7 6 5 4 3 2 1

This cookbook is dedicated to my family and friends
who have always been there to support me through every crazy idea
and leap of faith I take. I can't thank you enough!

Here's to the next chapter in our lives. I love you all so much.

xoxoxo
MDP

CONTENTS

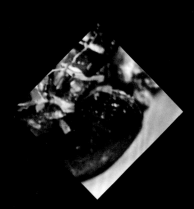

Clams
19

Mussels
89

Shrimp & Prawns
169

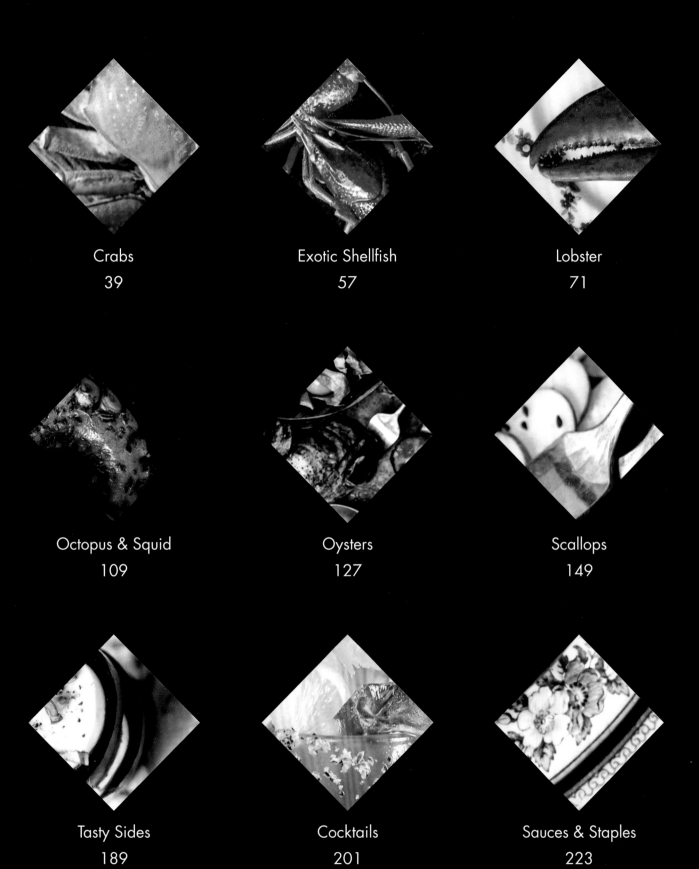

INTRO

HI, EVERYONE! I'm Chef Matt Dean Pettit, chef and co-owner and founder of Rock Lobster restaurants and Matty's Seafood Brands. Whether you've been to one of the restaurants, picked up some of our food from your local supermarket, or experimented in the kitchen with lobster recipes from my first cookbook, *The Great Lobster Cookbook*—or even if we've never crossed virtual or real-life paths before—you'll probably realize pretty quickly that seafood is one of my true loves and I keep it at the core of my daily life.

The Great Shellfish Cookbook takes any level of home cook on a delicious seafood tour that focuses on my personal top nine favorite kinds of shellfish. In much the same way as I demystified lobster in my first book, I'll teach you Shellfish 101 and show you how and where to buy fresh shellfish, how to store it, and, of course, how to cook it. We'll cook some fun and manageable types of shellfish, such as crab of different varieties, oysters, mussels, scallops, squid, octopus, clams, prawns, and, of course, lobster. And to help you bring it all

I knew, was that unless you have A LOT of money, it's almost impossible to have your own manufacturing facility to produce your own goods. Right away I understood that it was important to search out who could help co-pack and produce the products I intended to sell. At times the journey felt endless, although after researching for weeks, cold-calling manufacturing plants, and having countless doors shut in my face, I was able to find two amazing gentlemen who each owned large, federally inspected co-packing facilities. After several meetings and sales pitches, they finally agreed to take a chance on me. My determination paid off, and I felt on top of the world, as I'm sure you would have too.

After much blood, sweat, and tears, on January 1, 2014, I launched three products through Matty's Seafood Brands, in 12 Sobeys Urban Fresh stores in Toronto, Canada. The grocery game works quickly, and in less than 1 year, not only had we grown to four products—chowder, a lobster roll (an obvious choice as that's what we were best known for in our award-winning Rock Lobster restaurants), lobster mac 'n' cheese, and an amazing lobster bisque—but we had gone from 12 stores of distribution to approximately 275 throughout Ontario. And now? Our products are currently available in over 700+ stores across Canada and the United States, with a total of 10 Matty's Seafood Brands products—and growing—for you to enjoy! Right now, our products include lobster bisque, east coast chowder, mac 'n' cheese, sous vide lobster tails, scallops, and snow crabs, and a variety of seasoning mixes.

When I was a child, my mom taught me how to cook and showed me how to be creative, have fun, and express myself. I hope *The Great Shellfish Cookbook* helps you find your creative path and leads you on many food journeys, regardless of your travel budget. Here's to learning, cooking, and most importantly, eating delicious food with friends and family! Here's to some love, laughs, and happy cooking ahead!

Cheers!

Chef Matt Dean Pettit (MDP)

HOW TO USE THIS COOKBOOK

It's important to me that you understand how to buy, store, prepare, and cook the different types of shellfish so that you can fully enjoy all the flavors they offer! With that mind, do take the time to read and absorb the information in Shellfish 101. I can guarantee that it will save you time in the long run, will enhance your cooking experience, and will help you add that extra something to your finished dish.

I love to experiment with different shellfish as the seasons change and to use fresh local produce that's in season. In this cookbook, I draw on some of my recent exciting food travels to Japan, Thailand, Europe, and the southern United States for inspiration and guidance. We live in a global village, and the more we can share different recipes and cooking styles with one another, the more wonderful food we get to learn about and eat. But that doesn't mean that the recipes are complicated! I try to follow simple principles in my cooking: to always use fresh, beautiful ingredients; keep it simple; and cook from the heart and soul!

I've made a list of a few essential tools and ingredients that you'll find useful to keep on hand in case you return home from the grocery store laden with fresh shellfish and not much else. You'll see that this list is made up of things you probably keep in your pantry, or have on hand in the kitchen, most of the time. You can add to the list as you explore the world of shellfish cooking and discover new favorites, new staples, and new challenges.

As in my first book, *The Great Lobster Cookbook*, I've also included icons to help you decide at a glance what to make and when. Of course, there's nothing to stop you from having a brunch dish at dinner, or having dinner for breakfast, or even throwing yourself a party for one if the notion takes you!

ESSENTIAL TOOLS AND INGREDIENTS

Here are my top 10 essential ingredients and tools for
any shellfish lover to keep in the kitchen at all times:

1. Cast iron skillet
2. Nonstick skillet
3. Large sauté pan
4. Thin metal slotted spoon
5. Oyster knife

6. Chef's knife
7. Parchment paper
8. Good-quality canola oil
9. Fresh lemons and limes
10. Fresh herbs

ICONS

Below are some user-friendly icons that will guide you through which
dishes suit which occasions. A quick glance is all you'll need to know
when the recipe will be a winner. Icons are:

Brunch   Lunch   Dinner   Quick & Easy   Party!   Celeb Chef

Contributing celebrity chef recipes are dishes from my friends:

★ Guinness World Record holder for the most oysters shucked in 1 minute:
Patrick McMurray

★ The owner of an amazing Toronto-based seafood canning company, Scout Canning:
Charlotte Langley

★ World's youngest cheese master a.k.a. Batman a.k.a. our hero:
Afrim Pristine of Toronto's Cheese Boutique

SHELLFISH 101

In this section, I want to talk a little bit about the different kinds of shellfish you'll find mentioned throughout the book. In the following pages, you'll see a breakdown of each. But before we get started, there are a few general tips that I'd like to share with you too.

First off, some best practices:

- Always store shellfish in the lowest or coldest section of your fridge. I keep mine in the crisper drawer.
- Most types of shellfish shouldn't be submerged in water. There are a few occasions where a bath will help clean the shellfish, but your best bet is to follow the recipe directions carefully.
- Your shellfish should smell fresh, like the sea. If it seems off in any way, toss it.
- Be careful when seasoning shellfish. You want the natural flavor to shine through, and many types of shellfish have a salty taste from the ocean water.
- When buying frozen shellfish, keep an eye out for "glazing." This is when the manufacturer injects water into the shell to help protect the meat and potentially add more weight to the product. You can tell that a frozen shell has been glazed if it has a thick layer of shiny clear ice on it.
- Ask questions! Your fishmonger is a fountain of knowledge, and can help educate you on the different options available. This is especially important in terms of buying sustainable types of shellfish.

One reason I wanted to write this new cookbook was to educate readers on the importance of seafood sustainability. As the world's population grows larger each year, it's our shared responsibility to think consciously about preservation of the seafood we eat. For the health of our current and future generations, we must protect our global rivers, lakes, and oceans. But that doesn't mean that we can't enjoy seafood; we just need to think about how to do it in a responsible way.

There are several different organizations and accreditations that promote sustainably sourced shellfish. The two that I have worked with are the Marine Stewardship Council (MSC) and Ocean Wise. The MSC was founded in the U.K. in the mid-1990s. It's an independent, not-for-profit that promotes sustainability through the use of their blue eco-label, which you can see on certified shellfish and seafood products worldwide. The certification means that the product has been tracked and traced through a sustainable catch method, and sold through a sustainable fishery or retailer. You can learn more about the MSC at www.msc.org. Ocean Wise was founded in 2005 in Vancouver, British Columbia, as a conservation program through the Vancouver Aquarium. Like the MSC, Ocean Wise has a symbol that you can find on select seafood products that are sustainable and healthy for our oceans, as well as on certain restaurant menus too. This is especially helpful if you're celebrating a special occasion by dining out! You can learn more about Ocean Wise at www.ocean.org/seafood.

Both the MSC and Ocean Wise are fantastic organizations that help educate consumers, fishermen and -women, food processors, brands, retailers, restaurateurs, and everyone involved in the shellfish market as to what species it's okay to catch, and how to do so sustainably. If we all work together and pay attention to the health of our oceans, we can ensure that future generations have access to the same shellfish that we do today.

CLAMS

Clams are marine bivalve mollusks and are directly related to oysters and mussels; all are sustainable. They're great for the ocean because they can filter up to half a gallon (2 L) of water per day, removing excess algae and thus helping to clean and purify the water. There are over 15,000 species of clams, but in this book I've chosen to feature Ipswich clams (otherwise known as soft-shell clams, steamers, or longnecks), Manila clams (otherwise known as Japanese littlenecks), quahog clams (hard-shell clams also known as cherry stone, littlenecks, or top necks), and razor clams. These clams vary in taste and texture, ranging from sweet to salty to savory, and from soft to a little tougher—but they're all amazing to cook with (and eat, of course).

Clams are harvested by clam diggers who go out when the tide is low and use rakes to dig into the sand and mud and pull out the clams. Clams usually take 3 to 4 years to fully grow to maturation size, at which point they're ready to be sold.

When you're buying live, in-shell clams, be sure to smell the clams and check that they don't smell off (they should smell like the sea). If a clam is slightly open and you touch the shell and it closes right back up, that means that it's still alive and okay to eat. If it doesn't close but instead stays open, discard it.

Fun facts

The largest clam on record weighed 750 lb (340 kg) and was found in Japan in the late 1950s.

Clams can and some do produce pearls.

Clams cannot see, hear, or smell.

Clams need about 25–28 months of growth to reach legal selling size.

To store live, in-shell clams, keep them moist by wrapping them in a damp, wet dish towel or newspaper and storing them in the fridge. You don't want them to dry out, but don't submerge them in water either. Use these within 3 to 4 days, maximum.

CRABS

In this book, I use several species of crab. Despite my obsession with lobster, I have to tell you that crab is my all-time favorite shellfish because it's sweet in taste and light in texture, low in fat and calories, and a good source of protein.

Fun facts

The largest king crab in the world is the Japanese spider crab, which can reach 13 feet (156 inches) in length.

Blue crab is the most commonly consumed crab in the world.

Crabs communicate by flapping and moving their claws and pincers.

There are many types of crab species all over the world, but I want to focus on the ones that I know are sustainable. These include Atlantic snow and king crab from Alaska and Canada; and Dungeness crab, which is largely caught all along the west coast of Canada and the USA. Dungeness crabs are named after the town of Dungeness, in Washington State, which was the site of the first commercial crab fishery in North America, founded in 1848.

Crabs are caught in crab pots, which are 800 lb (360 kg) metal-framed traps that have various kinds of netting in them, depending on the type of crab being fished for. The pots that catch Alaskan king crabs are larger in size than the pots that catch Dungeness crab. Each crab pot has side holes that allow any bycatch (species caught in the trap that were not intended to be caught) to escape, making crab a viable sustainable shellfish option.

Many types of crab, such as Dungeness or blue crab, are available to buy live. King crab and snow crab are usually sold pre-cooked and as frozen legs. In any case, though, you can usually find crab all year long. To make it easier for yourself, you can also purchase crab meat that has been picked from its shell and sold as "lump crab meat." This is a great option when you're stuck for time. And if you're wondering what the difference between hard- and soft-shell crabs are, well, wonder no more! A soft-shell crab is simply a hard-shell crab that has shed its shell.

If you live near the ocean, you might have an easier time buying live crabs, especially when they're in season. Look for live crabs in tanks that aren't crowded and pick the ones that seem to have all their claws. Also, ensure they're active and not sluggish—this is a great rule of thumb when buying all shellfish.

To store live crabs, wrap them in a clean, damp dish towel or newspaper. They can then be stored in the refrigerator for 1 to 2 days.

Buying frozen pre-cooked crab legs is not always a bad way to go, as manufacturers commonly flash-freeze the crab legs, locking in the flavors. Use caution when buying frozen crab legs, though, and especially for king crab, as retailers or processors will sometimes glaze the meat.

Frozen crab legs can be stored in the freezer for up to 6 months. Once they've thawed out, use them within 2 days. Do not refreeze them.

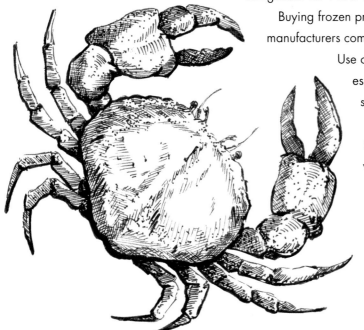

EXOTIC SHELLFISH

Some types of shellfish don't always get the same amount of love as the others. You may not have heard of the shellfish listed below, or perhaps you've just never tried them. Now's the time to taste something new and expand your shellfish horizons!

Conch

Conch (pronounced "konk") are hand-harvested, but have been removed from a lot of sustainability lists as stock levels have dropped in places like the Bahamas, Bermuda, and the Florida Keys where they're a staple. So, be sure to only buy conch from a reputable fishmonger or shellfish purveyor, who can help educate you on conch sustainability.

Fun facts

As conch get older, their shells become thicker.

Conch meat is said to be a natural aphrodisiac.

Farming conch has recently become popular in order to help rebuild stock levels and boost sustainability.

Conch can be switched out for lobster (they're known as the "poor man's lobster") if desired, but the conch will be a bit tougher. The meat is best prepared by tenderizing it with a mallet or by breaking it down in citrus. It can be tough to get their meat out, and they certainly make you work for your food, but when you succeed, you'll find that they're extremely tasty.

Conch should only be purchased live, like mollusks. To store live conch, wrap them in a damp dish towel or newspapers and keep them in the refrigerator for 3 to 4 days.

Crawfish

Crawfish are crustaceans, like lobster; in fact, they're related. Crawfish from Louisiana are fully sustainable, as you'll seldom find live crawfish outside of the southern USA.

As with most crustaceans, make sure that you don't submerge them in water or dump ice on them. It's better to keep them just damp, as ice can quickly kill live shellfish. Store crawfish in a cooler with damp dish towels for a couple of hours. If you need to store them for a longer period, place them in a large container with breathing holes, and refrigerate them for up to 2 days.

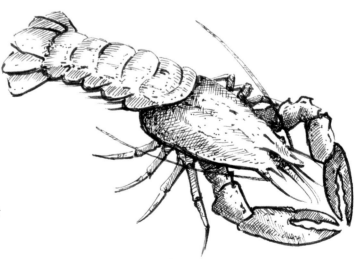

Fun facts

The state of Louisiana supplies close to 95% of the world's crawfish supply.

Crawfish are also known as "mud bugs" and come in various colors: pink, red, white, blue, and brown.

When eating crawfish, have a lot of fun with them. Don't get discouraged by the small amount of meat in each one. What it lacks in quantity is more than compensated for by quality—it's incredibly sweet. My favorite part of eating crawfish is sucking the juice from the head.

Periwinkles

Periwinkles are sea snails and are part of the mollusk family. Like conch, they can be difficult when it comes to removing the meat, but they're absolutely delicious. Periwinkles are sweet and briny—they taste like the sea. They're a good source of protein and very easy to cook. Most of them are still hand-harvested, like conch, and therefore the harvesting makes almost no impact on their ecosystem.

Fun facts

In medieval England, you could buy periwinkles for a penny per handful or two pennies per pound, making them one of the cheapest types of shellfish available.

Periwinkles are found on beaches, on rocks, and in the mud, making them very easy to harvest.

Unlike most marine animals, periwinkles can survive in fresh water.

Periwinkles should only be purchased live, like all mollusks. To store live periwinkles, wrap them in a damp dish towel or newspaper and keep them in the refrigerator for 3 to 4 days.

Sea Urchin

A sea urchin's eggs, or "uni" as they're called in Japanese, are a real delicacy. If you've ever tried to open a sea urchin, you know it takes practice, but like anything, practice makes perfect. When you cut into the sea urchin, it will still be alive and the quills will be moving slightly. To prepare it for cooking, you drive a knife into the center, trim the quills, and remove the top shell—think of carving a pumpkin. The sea urchin will then be open, and you'll be able to access each of the five segments of uni. The uni (bright yellow-orange colored meat) is creamy in texture and sweet in taste.

Fun facts

Sea urchins are also known as "sea hedgehogs."

Sea urchins can live to be 200 years old.

When buying live sea urchins, ensure that they're intact and not damaged or cracked.

To store live sea urchins, place them in a large container with breathing holes, and refrigerate them for up to 1 week.

LOBSTERS

There are 48 known types of lobsters throughout the world. The three that most people know are North American lobster, spiny Caribbean/rock lobster, and European lobster.

Most of what we see in North America is from the Eastern seaboard, from up and down the coasts of Canada and the USA. These North American lobsters are green-brown in color, and have claws and tails full of meat. Spiny Caribbean or rock lobsters have most of their meat located in their tails and are found in warm waters near Mexico, Australia, New Zealand, and the Caribbean islands. The European lobster is usually blue and is smaller than North American or rock lobsters.

In terms of sustainability, lobster is in a good place. Governing boards are firmly controlling and enforcing trap sizes, as well as fishing season times. There is also a minimum weight requirement for a caught lobster. They must weigh at least 1 lb (450 g) (which takes about 6 to 7 years) to be considered legal fishing size.

The key to buying lobster (and, in fact, all shellfish) is to remember that when you weigh them, you must account for the weight in the shell, which you won't be eating. It will be important to purchase enough of the seafood to ensure you have the amount required for each recipe. For example, a lobster that is called a "quarter" and weighs 1¼ lb (560 g) will only have about 6 oz (170 g) of pure meat in it.

Remember too that more than just the lobster meat can be enjoyed. Consider using the coral or roe (little red eggs from within a female lobster) in your next recipe; some even consider the liver (the green matter) to be a delicacy.

When buying whole, live lobsters, look for lobsters that move around a lot in the tank—you don't want the sluggish ones. Never purchase from any tanks that have murky water and are over-crowded with lobsters or other shellfish. Always purchase from a fishmonger who goes through a fairly large volume to ensure you're getting fresh product.

To store live lobsters, place them in the lowest spot in your refrigerator, because this is where it's nice and cold, but not freezing. Cover them in damp dish towels or news-paper, and make sure to keep the lobsters damp at all times. Replace the towels when needed. Store in the refrigerator for up to 2 days.

When buying frozen lobster tails, watch for glazing, which appears as a thick clear ice on the shell, and don't buy lobsters that look glazed. Purchase tails that are in sealed packages in good shape, and where the meat looks white in the shells and not brown-yellow in color. Check out our Matty's Seafood

Lobster tail—it's raw, and we do all the hard work for you by peeling and shelling the tail.

Thaw out lobster tails overnight in the refrigerator or place them under cold, running water for 30 minutes, or until thawed. Do not refreeze them.

When buying previously cooked lobster meat, ensure that the meat still smells fresh and isn't too loose and crumbly (as this indicates it's old and off).

To store previously cooked lobster meat, put it in an airtight container in the refrigerator and use within 2 days.

Fun facts

The largest lobster ever caught was almost 44 ½ lb (20 kg) in Nova Scotia, Canada, in 1977.

Lobsters were once fed to prisoners, until they revolted and demanded different food.

If a lobster loses a claw or pincher, it can regrow it over time.

MUSSELS

These bivalve mollusks are part of the same family as oysters and clams. Mussels, like oysters, are grown and farmed by humans (and aquaculture, the farming of mussels in human-controlled conditions). Mussels are great for the environment as they filter our oceans, freshwater rivers, and lakes, which makes them one of the highest-ranked sustainable shellfish you can eat.

Mussels start out as small seeds or spat, which are hard shells. At around 1 year old, the mussel seeds will become large enough for the farmer to sort, and grade into sizes. Most commonly, the mussels are then put into individual mesh sleeves called "socks" and are tied to long ropes floating in the water. That said, mussels can be grown in a couple of different ways, including rope culture and raft culture. Rope culture, which is most common in France, is when long poles are dug into the shoreline and a net is essentially wrapped around the pole. The farmers maintain that netting as the mussels grow and come to harvest. Raft culture is another popular farming method, whereby a raft that has several mesh sacks hangs from it into the water underneath, allowing the spat to develop into mussels. Both of these methods have their pros and cons, and each mussel farmer has their own preference, but I've been told consistently that the most important component for great mussels is clean water.

When it's time to shop for mussels, you'll see that they're always sold with specification tags telling you where they're from and when they were harvested. There are several ways to prepare mussels, as you'll see in this cookbook. The most important part of cooking them is to make sure to check for any shells that did not open, before you plate your dish. Any mussels that haven't opened must be discarded.

When you're buying live mussels, ensure that they smell fresh like the ocean, and not off or stinky. It's not bad to buy them with the beards still

Fun facts

Mussels release water and liquid when steaming, therefore you don't need to add a lot of water when cooking them.

Mussels can live up for to 50 years and have been a food source for over 2,000 years.

Mussels can filter approximately 17 gallons (65 L) of water per day.

on them as they'll have a longer life span since they will tend to stay closed more easily. If you're buying them in 1 lb (450 g) or 2 lb (900 g) bags, ask your fishmonger when they came out of the water. They should still have a tag with that information on it. Within a week is ideal, but not mandatory.

Discard any shells that are broken or open prior to cooking. Store the live mussels in the refrigerator wrapped in damp dish towels or newspaper to keep them moist. As with other mollusks and bivalves, never submerge or store them in water. Correctly stored, mussels should last 3 to 4 days in your refrigerator.

OCTOPUSES & SQUIDS

If you're wondering why octopuses and squids fit into the shellfish category, wonder no more! They are part of the mollusk family and are called cephalopods. This means they have a prominent head and sets of arms or tentacles, and (most) can shoot ink. However, octopuses and squids are not born with shells and don't develop shells during their life.

Both octopuses and squids live in hot, tropical, saltwater climates. Many octopuses are harvested using ocean-bottom trawling, which can easily catch unwanted species (called bycatch) so it's important to ask your fishmonger or retailer if you're buying sustainably sourced octopus. There are great options, such as wild octopuses from Spain and Portugal, that are caught in pots or traps and are sustainably certified.

Squids, on the other hand, are harvested using the jigger method. A bright light is directed into the deep water of the ocean, which attracts the squids. Once they're in open water, they're trapped with nets.

When you're buying fresh, whole octopuses, ensure that they're not leaking their juices and that they're still moist. Ideally, look for smaller octopuses between 1 ½ lb (680 g) and 3 lb (1.3 kg), as their flavor is better. To store fresh, whole octopuses, keep them damp and covered with a damp dish towel or newspaper in the refrigerator. Make sure to use them within 1 to 2 days.

When you're buying frozen, whole octopuses, look for ones that have not been glazed—where they have a thick, clear layer of ice on the shell—or are freezer burnt. When storing frozen, whole octopuses, keep them frozen until needed and thaw in the fridge for 12 to 24 hours prior to use.

When you're buying fresh, whole squids, you want to buy squids that have already been cleaned; you may need to ask your fishmonger to do so. Look for squids that are a nice white color and not off-white or blue-yellow. When storing fresh, whole

Fun facts

There are more than 300 types of squid.

Some squid can reach up to 1,000 lb (450 kg).

Octopuses can camouflage themselves in a matter of seconds to blend into the ocean floor.

squids, wrap them in a damp dish towel or newspaper and refrigerate them for up to 2 days. Check to ensure that the smell has not gone off before eating.

When you're buying fresh, frozen squid, be careful not to pay for too much frozen water weight. This can happen with any frozen shellfish, so be alert and ask questions. A good fishmonger will be happy to help you and to answer your questions. To store fresh, frozen squid, keep them frozen until needed. Thaw overnight in the fridge and use within 1 day. Do not store thawed-out squid.

OYSTERS

Oysters are one of the most sustainable types of shellfish in the world, as nearly 95% of all the oysters that we eat are farmed by harvesters. Oysters (otherwise known as bivalve mollusks, which means having two shells) act as a filter because they process water through their gills, helping to clean the water they live in—just as mussels do.

Oyster farmers, like wine makers, can adjust their process and make a difference in how the final oyster products are developed. First, oysters are grown on oyster beds that can be customized to affect the size of the oyster: small cocktail size, larger standard size, shallow cup, or deep cup. Natural elements such as ocean water, saltiness of the ocean, area predators, and weather conditions are vital factors affecting the growth and success of an oyster's development. Oyster farmers will take their oysters on-shore for a period of time, allowing them to grow on land and develop further, before returning them to the water to mature. Again cold, clean pristine water is key to the success of the oyster, which is why North America's northern east coast makes for a perfect habitat.

Oysters are a fantastic source of calcium, zinc, and iron, and have become very popular over the years in countries such as Canada, the USA, and Japan.

Fun facts

Oysters sometimes have both male and female genes.

To some people's dismay, oysters are not a natural aphrodisiac.

The world's largest oyster was 14 inches (35.5 cm) long.

Buy live oysters that have dates (showing when they were removed from the water) on them or ask your fishmonger for this information. Smell the oysters before buying them. If they have a strong pungent smell, do not buy them.

Do not store in-shell oysters in water. You should rinse them to wash off any excess mud or dirt, but that's it—do not submerge them. Eat the oysters within 1 week of buying them. Keep them in the refrigerator, covered with damp paper towels so they stay damp. Replace the towel if necessary.

When you're buying pre-shucked oysters, make sure to purchase containers that are vacuum-packed and sealed. Check that the oysters are still fresh by referring to the use-by date on the package, and smell them once you open it.

Once a package of pre-shucked oysters has been opened, use them all at once. Do not store any uneaten oysters.

SCALLOPS

The word "scallop" refers to the meat inside the bivalve mollusks. In this book, I use bay scallops, sea scallops, and the harder-to-come-by diver scallops.

Bay scallops are much smaller than any other scallop and are sweet. They're perfect for sautéing. Sea scallops are large, ranging from 1 to 2 inches (2.5 to 5 cm) in width, and are perfect for searing. Diver scallops are like sea scallops, but have been hand-harvested from the ocean floor by scuba divers. Due to cost and many other factors, apparently only about 1% of the scallops that we eat are actually "diver caught."

Fun facts

Marco Polo first recorded that scallops were for sale in Hangchow, China, in 1280.

Scallops can never fully close their shells, unlike clams, mussels, and oysters.

Scallops are rich in omega-3 fatty acid and are a fabulous source of protein.

Scallops are generally harvested using dredges or bottom trowels. Sea scallops, for example, are shucked and chill-stored on the fishing boat as they need water to live. All types of scallops should be marked in your local fish store with 10/20, 20/30 or 30/40, all of which refer to the number of scallops per pound. Alternatively, scallops may be sold with a "U" such as U10, which means that you're buying fewer than 10 scallops per pound. This gives you an idea of the size and quantity of scallops that you're buying.

Fresh scallops should smell like the sea and have no off-putting odor. Press down on the scallop with your fingers. The meat should rebound quickly into place. Try to buy scallops that are bright white in color, from a fishmonger who you trust. Some processors can shoot them with a solution called STP (sodium tripolyphosphate) to keep them from browning and drying out. The issue here is scallops that have STP in them will also hold more excess moisture, which shrinks them by more than 50% when cooked. Your fishmonger will be able to guide you.

To store fresh scallops, wrap them in a damp dish towel or newspaper and refrigerate them for up to 2 days. They don't keep very long, so it's actually better to cook them the day you buy them.

When you're buying frozen scallops, do not buy any packages that are damaged, opened, or spoiled in any way. Avoid packages that have noticeable ice crystals, as this could mean that the package has been thawed and refrozen several times.

Thaw frozen scallops overnight in the fridge before use and store them in the refrigerator for 1 to 2 days. If you want to sear them, make sure that you pat them dry first.

SHRIMP & PRAWNS

The shellfish category of shrimp and prawns is important to discuss in detail because there's a dark side to the commercial shrimping industry.

Most of the shrimp we purchase as consumers come from the eastern hemisphere, and it's worth remembering that, in many cases, the companies that harvest these shrimp have employee health and safety standards that differ from those in North America. Their sustainability practices can vary widely from ours as well.

For these reasons, I chose to focus on sustainably sourced wild shrimp from Florida; side stripe shrimp from coastal inlets of British Columbia, Canada; and legendary spot prawns, which have short seasonal availability, can be eaten raw, and are from the west coasts of the United States and Canada.

The difference between shrimp and prawns can seem confusing, but with a closer look it's easy to see. Shrimp have branching gills, and prawns have lamellate gills that look as though they're little, overlapping plates. Prawns are generally—but not always—larger, with bigger legs, and claws on three pairs. Shrimp are generally smaller, with claws on two pairs of their shorter legs.

Fun facts

Shrimp and prawns can range from ½ inch to 12 inches (1.2 cm to 30 cm) in size.

Shrimp and prawns are a good source of protein and low in calories, with an average of 7 calories per item when cooked.

Shrimp and prawns, like fish, generally travel in schools.

When purchasing shrimp or prawns from your fishmonger, ask them a few questions to ensure that the product is of a high quality and sustainably sourced. It's important that you learn where the shrimp or prawns are from, whether they're fresh or frozen, and if they were wild or farmed. Both wild and farmed shrimp and prawns have positives and negatives. For example, a lot of farmed shrimp is better in most cases for sustainability, although some shrimp are, unfortunately, grown and harvested in murky, dirty waters.

When you're buying fresh shrimp and prawns, ensure that their eyes, if you're buying them with their heads on, are clear and not cloudy. If buying them live, buy the ones that are not damaged or missing legs, and are full of movement. Ensure they smell fresh and not off. If the shrimp don't have their heads on, make sure that the meat is firm and plump, without any odor. Try not to buy shrimp or prawns that have been pre-peeled or have discolored yellow meat or brown markings, as these are all signifiers of age.

Store fresh shrimp and prawns in an airtight container in the refrigerator for up to 5 days. Add 1 tsp (5 mL) of fresh lemon juice to extend their freshness.

When buying frozen shrimp and prawns, purchase ones that have not been glazed, which leaves a thick, clear, icy layer on the shell. Thaw them in the refrigerator overnight and use within 2 days of thawing.

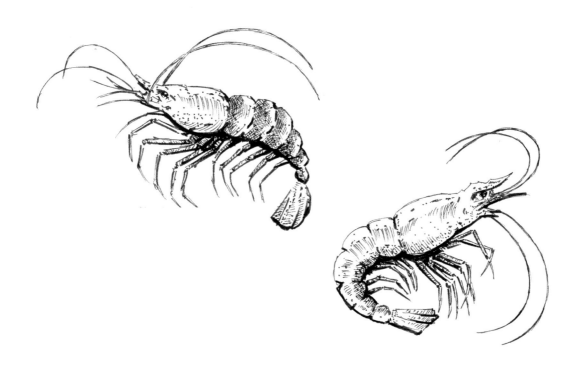

CLAMS

Brunch

SERVES 6–8

1 lb (450 g) live Ipswich clams

¼ cup (60 mL) unsalted butter, melted

8 medium eggs

1 cup (250 mL) double-smoked bacon, cut into ½-inch (1.2 cm) cubes

½ cup (125 mL) diced Spanish onion

½ cup (125 mL) asparagus, cut into 1½-inch (4 cm) pieces

½ cup (125 mL) diced red bell pepper

½ cup (125 mL) 1% milk

Kosher salt and freshly ground black pepper

BACON & CLAM MINI FRITTATAS

This timeless and simple dish is perfect for breakfast or brunch any day of the week. Try making these frittatas a day ahead of time and storing them in an airtight container in the refrigerator so they're ready when you are. The addition of the bacon makes this dish absolutely mouthwatering.

1. Preheat the oven to 375°F (190°C). 2. Rinse the clams under cold, running water and pull off any hair to debeard them. 3. In a large saucepan, bring 4 cups (1 L) of cold water to a boil over high heat. Place the clams in the boiling water and cook for 3 to 5 minutes, or until they've fully opened. Using a slotted spoon, remove the clams from the water and discard any that did not open. Once the clams have cooled enough to handle, carefully remove the top shell from one clam at a time, using your fingers. Hold a clam in the palm of your hand and grip it tightly with your fingers. Then, using a paring knife, slip the knife under the clam meat to loosen the lower adductors, allowing you to remove the meat. Roughly chop the meat, set it aside and discard the shells. 4. Grease the cups of a 12-cup muffin pan with the melted butter. 5. In a large bowl, whisk the eggs and then fold in the clam meat, bacon, onions, asparagus, bell peppers, milk, and salt and pepper to taste. 6. Pour the egg mixture into the muffin pan. Place the pan in the oven and bake for 25 to 35 minutes, or until a knife inserted into the center of a frittata comes out clean. 7. Allow the frittatas to cool for 10 to 15 minutes. Remove from the muffin pan, serve, and enjoy!

Party!

SERVES 2–4

2 lb (900 g) quahog clams

1 cup (250 mL) chickpea flour

1 ½ tsp (7 mL) kosher salt

1 tsp (5 mL) cayenne pepper

½ tsp (2 mL) smoked paprika

½ tsp (2 mL) brown sugar

Freshly ground black pepper

4 large egg whites

½ cup (125 mL) 2% milk

1 cup (250 mL) canola oil

½ cup (125 mL) hot sauce
(I like Frank's RedHot Sauce)

2 Tbsp (30 mL) unsalted butter,
melted

½ cup (125 mL) ranch dipping
sauce, for serving

BUFFALO FRIED CLAMS

Anyone who knows me well knows that I'm a die-hard Buffalo Bills and NFL fan.

In the past, I've been hired by the NFL to work as their Super Bowl Chef, and I've been fortunate enough to make great game day recipes like this one. This recipe honors the city that is not only home to the Buffalo Bills but also the birthplace of Buffalo chicken wings. Whether you're a football fan or not, grab a cold beer and lots of creamy ranch sauce. This recipe doubles easily and can be scaled up to feed a crowd.

1. Rinse the clams under cold, running water and pull off any hair to debeard them. 2. In a large saucepan, bring 4 cups (1 L) of cold water to a boil over high heat. Place the clams in the boiling water and cook for 3 to 5 minutes, or until they've fully opened. Using a slotted spoon, remove the clams from the water and discard any that did not open. Once the clams have cooled enough to handle, remove the top shell from one clam at a time, using your fingers. Hold a clam in the palm of your hand and grip it tightly. Then, using a paring knife, slip the knife under the clam meat to loosen the lower adductors, allowing you to remove the meat, keeping it intact. Set the meat aside and discard the shells. 3. Set up a dredging station. In a small, shallow bowl, combine the flour, salt, cayenne pepper, paprika, brown sugar, and a pinch of black pepper. In a separate shallow bowl, whisk the egg whites and milk together. 4. Dip the clam meats, one at a time, into the egg mixture, and then into the flour mixture. Repeat this step to ensure they're fully coated. Set the coated clam meats aside on a plate until you're ready to fry them. 5. In a medium-size saucepan, heat the canola oil over medium-high heat. If the oil begins to boil, turn down the heat to bring it to a simmer. Line a plate with paper towels. 6. Work in small batches and allow the oil to come back up to temperature in between each batch. Using tongs, carefully place the coated clams in the hot oil. Don't crowd the pan. Fry for 2 to 3 minutes, or until they float to the top and are golden brown. Using a slotted spoon, transfer the clams to the prepared plate to absorb any excess oil. Repeat until all the clams are fried, crispy, and golden brown. 7. In a medium-size bowl, combine the hot sauce and melted butter. Toss the fried clams into the hot sauce mixture, ensuring they're evenly coated, and serve hot, with ranch dipping sauce.

Quick & Easy

SERVES 4–6

1 lb (450 g) live Ipswich clams

1 lb (450 g) smoked strip bacon, cut into ½-inch (1.2 cm) cubes

½ cup (125 mL) diced celery

½ cup (125 mL) diced white onion

½ cup (125 mL) diced carrots

1 sprig fresh thyme

Kosher salt and freshly ground black pepper

1 bottle (355 mL) beer (any kind you wish)

1 cup (250 mL) clam juice, store-bought or reserved liquor from the clams

1 Tbsp (15 mL) cornstarch

2 cups (500 mL) finely diced Yukon Gold potatoes

1 cup (250 mL) heavy (35%) cream

1 tsp (5 mL) cayenne pepper

NOTE: Skip the beer and replace with water to make this recipe gluten-free.

CLAM CHOWDER

This is my favorite chowder because it's so easy to make. Putting it into the slow cooker or crock pot is such a timesaver, leaving you more time in your day for a little R&R.

This recipe is one of our top-selling products at Matty's Seafood. If you're looking for a few other ways to use chowder, try it as a base for a seafood pasta sauce or as a "gravy" with warm biscuits.

1. Rinse the clams under cold, running water and pull off any hair to debeard them. 2. In a large saucepan, bring 4 cups (1 L) of cold water to a boil over high heat. Place the clams in the boiling water and cook for 3 to 5 minutes, or until they've fully opened. Using a slotted spoon, remove the clams from the water and discard any that did not open. Once the clams have cooled enough to handle, carefully remove the top shell from one clam at a time, using your fingers. Hold a clam in the palm of your hand and grip it tightly with your fingers. Then, using a paring knife, slip the knife under the clam meat to loosen the lower adductors, allowing you to remove the meat. Set the meat aside in the fridge and discard the shells. 3. In a slow cooker, place the bacon, celery, onions, carrots, thyme, and salt and pepper to taste with the beer and clam juice. Stir well. Cook, covered, on high for 10 to 15 minutes, or until the vegetables are soft. 4. In a small bowl, whisk the cornstarch with 2 Tbsp (30 mL) of cold water to create a slurry. This will prevent the cornstarch from clumping in the soup base. Add the cornstarch slurry and 4 cups (1 L) of cold water to the slow cooker. Keep the heat on high, and give the soup a big stir. Add the potatoes, cover with the lid, and bring to a boil. Reduce the heat to low, and allow the chowder to simmer for 15 to 20 minutes. 5. Finally, add the clam meat, heavy cream, and cayenne pepper, and stir to combine. Check the seasoning and add more salt and pepper if desired. 6. Cook on low for 2 to 3 hours. 7. Serve with Quick & Easy No-Knead Beer Bread (page 194) to soak up the soup!

Party!

SERVES 4–6

12 live razor clams

2 shallots, finely diced

2 Serrano chilies, seeded and finely diced

½ cup (125 mL) finely diced English cucumber (skin on)

½ cup (125 mL) fresh lime juice (about 4 limes)

1 Tbsp (15 mL) agave nectar

2 medium avocados

Kosher salt, to taste

1 small bunch cilantro leaves, stems discarded

1 Tbsp (15 mL) chili powder, for garnish

Tortilla chips, for serving

RAZOR CLAM CEVICHE

The first time I ate razor clams I was at an incredible restaurant just off the Champs-Élysées in Paris with some friends of mine from the wine business. The clams were so delicate and perfectly prepared that night. After that, I wanted to learn more about them. They may look unusual to many people, but trust me, you should give them a try. This recipe can be scaled up easily for a larger crowd.

1. Rinse the clams under cold, running water and pull off any hair to debeard them. Transfer them to a large bowl and pour hot, but not boiling, water over them. Keep them submerged for a few minutes so the shells start to open. Once all the shells have opened, transfer them to another bowl filled with cold water to stop them from cooking, and discard any clams that didn't open. Finally, using a small paring knife, carefully open the clams, remove the meat from the shell, remove and discard the digestive track (it looks like the vein of a shrimp) and roughly chop the meat. Set the meat aside in the fridge and discard the shells. 2. In a medium-size bowl, place ½ cup (125 mL) cold water with the shallots, chilies, cucumbers, lime juice, and agave nectar. Then add the reserved clam meat. Mix well, cover, and then refrigerate for 1 to 2 hours to allow the flavors to mingle. 3. Cut the avocados into ½-inch (1.2 cm) cubes. Add them to the clam meat and gently mix them together. Strain off any excess liquid and season to taste with salt. Transfer the ceviche into small serving bowls. Garnish with cilantro and a sprinkle of chili powder and serve with tortilla chips.

Brunch

SERVES 2–4

1 lb (450 g) Ipswich clams

¼ cup (60 mL) unsalted butter, melted

6 medium eggs

1 cup (250 mL) fresh spinach, stems removed

1 cup (250 mL) finely chopped fresh kale, stems removed

1 cup (250 mL) shredded Swiss cheese

½ cup (125 mL) grated Parmigiano-Reggiano cheese

½ cup (125 mL) diced white onion

½ cup (125 mL) diced on-the-vine tomatoes

1 Tbsp (15 mL) smoked paprika

NOTE: This also makes a great dinner dish, served with a big green salad.

CRUSTLESS CLAM QUICHE

This easy-to-make crustless quiche has all the elements of a great-tasting dish: saltiness from the cheeses, sweetness from the clams, and acidity from the tomatoes. Combine these flavors with the beautiful texture of the baked eggs and you're all set!

1. Preheat the oven to 375°F (190°C). **2.** Rinse the clams under cold, running water and pull off any hair to debeard them. **3.** In a large saucepan, bring 4 cups (1 L) of cold water to a boil over high heat. Place the clams in the boiling water and cook for 3 to 5 minutes, or until they've fully opened. Using a slotted spoon, remove the clams from the water and discard any that did not open. Once the clams have cooled enough to handle, carefully remove the top shell from one clam at a time, using your fingers. Hold a clam in the palm of your hand and grip it tightly with your fingers. Then, using a paring knife, slip the knife under the clam meat to loosen the lower adductors, allowing you to remove the meat. Roughly chop the meat, set it aside and discard the shells. **4.** Grease a medium-size, about 10-inch (25 cm), round pie plate or oven-safe baking dish with the melted butter. **5.** In a large mixing bowl, whisk the eggs and then fold in the clam meat, spinach, kale, both cheeses, onions, tomatoes, and paprika, making sure everything is well combined. **6.** Pour the egg mixture into the greased pie plate and bake for 30 to 35 minutes, or until a knife inserted into the center comes out clean. **7.** Remove the dish from the oven and allow the quiche to cool for 10 to 15 minutes. Cut into squares to serve.

Party!

SERVES 6–8

24 littleneck clams

½ cup (125 mL) dry white wine

3 Tbsp (45 mL) unsalted butter, melted

Juice from 1 lemon

¼ cup (60 mL) chopped fresh flat-leaf parsley

4 cloves garlic, minced

8 slices strip bacon, cut into ½-inch (1.2 cm) cubes

1 cup (250 mL) grated Parmigiano-Reggiano cheese

Lemon wedges, for serving

CLAMS CASINO

I absolutely love this dish. Over the years, I've had the chance to perfect it, as my catering company was tasked in 2014 with providing food for a large fundraising event and we've been providing it for them ever since. The event organizer swears by Clams Casino and insisted from the beginning that I include it on my menu. Now it's time for you to try your hand at it! This is also a great gluten-free recipe.

1. Preheat the oven to 375°F (190°C). 2. Rinse the clams under cold, running water and pull off any hair to debeard them. 3. On a baking tray, lay the clams in a single layer. Bake the clams for 5 to 7 minutes, or until they've opened. Carefully remove the clams from the oven, leaving the oven on. If any clams did not open, simply discard them and their liquid. 4. Gently insert a small paring knife into the hinge of the clam shell to separate the top and bottom shells. Remove the top portion of the shell, and loosen the meat using the knife. Leave the meat sitting inside its bottom shell. Repeat with the remaining clams, putting them back on the baking tray once you've done so. 5. In a small bowl, combine the white wine, melted butter, and lemon juice with the parsley and garlic. Stir well, and set aside. 6. Spoon a little bit of the butter mixture into each clam half. Top each clam with a few pieces of bacon and a healthy pinch of grated Parmigiano-Reggiano. Bake the clams for 5 to 7 minutes, or until the mixture is brown and bubbling. 7. Serve immediately with lemon wedges on the side.

Dinner

SERVES 2-4

1 lb (450 g) live Manila clams

2 lb (900 g) fresh pizza
   dough, store-bought or
   homemade

Cornmeal, for dusting

½ cup (125 mL) tomato sauce

1 head garlic, roasted (see
   note)

2 medium Roma tomatoes,
   thinly sliced

6 slices prosciutto

1 cup (250 mL) shredded
   mozzarella cheese

1 cup (250 mL) baby arugula

Juice from ½ large lemon

NOTE: For a quick and easy
way to roast garlic, preheat
the oven to 400°F (200°C).
Using a sharp knife, slice off
just the top of the bulb of
garlic, exposing the tops of
each clove. Season with salt,
pepper, and a sprinkle of good
olive oil, and bake for 15 to
20 minutes, or until soft and
brown. Let cool and then slide
each clove out of its skin and
add a super-sweet note to
your dish!

MATTY'S MANILA CLAM PIZZA

Manila clams, otherwise known as Japanese littlenecks, are originally from Asia and were first brought over to North America in the early 1930s. Believe it or not, they were mistakenly packed and shipped with oyster seeds—a happy accident, as far as I'm concerned.

These plump and meaty clams are ideal for this recipe as they add the perfect texture and sweetness. Try this and see for yourself!

1. Rinse the clams under cold, running water and pull off any hair to debeard them. 2. In a large saucepan, bring 4 cups (1 L) of cold water to a boil over high heat. Place the clams in the boiling water and cook for 3 to 5 minutes, or until they've fully opened. Using a slotted spoon, remove the clams from the water and discard any that did not open. Once the clams have cooled enough to handle, carefully remove the top shell from one clam at a time, using your fingers. Hold a clam in the palm of your hand and grip it tightly with your fingers. Then, using a paring knife, slip the knife under the clam meat to loosen the lower adductors, allowing you to remove the meat. Roughly chop the meat and set it aside in the fridge. Discard the shells. 3. Bring the pizza dough to room temperature, which should take 15 to 20 minutes. Meanwhile, preheat the oven to 425°F (220°C). 4. Using a rolling pin and a little bit of cornmeal on a large clean surface, roll the dough out until it's ¼-inch (6 mm) thick and 12 inches (30 cm) round. 5. Place the dough on a pizza stone or a large oval baking tray with a pinch of cornmeal on the bottom. Spoon the tomato sauce onto the middle of the dough and use the back of a spoon to smooth it out toward the edges, covering the entire pizza base. Lay the roasted garlic pieces, tomato slices, and prosciutto evenly overtop. 6. Bake the pizza for 6 to 8 minutes, or until the crust is starting to crisp and turn brown. 7. Remove the pizza from the oven, leaving the oven switched on, and evenly distribute the clam meat and cheese over it. Place the pizza back in the oven and bake for another 4 to 5 minutes, or until the cheese is golden brown and bubbling. 8. Remove the pizza from the oven, garnish with the arugula, and sprinkle with the lemon juice. Cut the pizza into slices and serve immediately.

Lunch

SERVES 2

1 lb (450 g) quahog clams

2 Tbsp (30 mL) salted butter

2 Tbsp (30 mL) all-purpose flour

2 cups (500 mL) 2% milk

1 Tbsp (15 mL) ground nutmeg

Kosher salt and freshly ground black pepper

2 cups (500 mL) shredded aged white cheddar cheese, divided

3 cups (750 mL) elbow macaroni noodles

¾ cup (175 mL) Panko breadcrumbs

QUAHOG CLAM MAC & CHEESE

Lobster Mac & Cheese is tasty and fun to make, but with the rising costs of live lobster and lobster meat, I wanted to give you an equally delicious—and less expensive—alternative! If clams aren't your thing, try switching them out for oysters, crab, or mussels.

1. Rinse the clams under cold, running water and pull off any hair to debeard them. 2. In a large saucepan, bring 4 cups (1 L) of cold water to a boil over high heat. Place the clams in the boiling water and cook for 3 to 5 minutes, or until they've fully opened. Using a slotted spoon, remove the clams from the water and discard any that did not open. Once the clams have cooled enough to handle, carefully remove the top shell from one clam at a time, using your fingers. Hold a clam in the palm of your hand and grip it tightly with your fingers. Then, using a paring knife, slip the knife under the clam meat to loosen the lower adductors, allowing you to remove the meat. Coarsely chop the meat and place it in a bowl. Cover and set aside in the refrigerator until needed. Discard the shells. 3. Preheat the oven to 375°F (190°C). 4. In a large saucepan, melt the butter over medium heat. Add the flour and cook, stirring, for approximately 1 minute. Whisk in the milk gradually until the mixture is smooth. Bring the ingredients to a simmer, continuing to whisk until the mixture has thickened. Sprinkle with the nutmeg and a pinch of salt and pepper. Stir in 1 cup (250 mL) of the cheese until it has melted and the sauce is smooth. 5. Meanwhile, in a medium-size saucepan of boiling salted water, cook the pasta for 4 to 5 minutes, or until al dente. Drain the pasta and transfer it to the cheese sauce. Add the clam meat. Mix thoroughly to combine. 6. Transfer the pasta and sauce to a 9-inch (23 cm) square oven-safe dish. Top with the breadcrumbs and remaining cheese. Bake for 12 to 15 minutes, or until the cheese is bubbly and brown. Serve immediately.

Lunch

SERVES 2–4

1 lb (450 g) live razor clams

4 Tbsp (60 mL) extra-virgin olive oil, divided

¼ cup (60 mL) dry white wine

4 green onions, finely chopped

2 cloves garlic, minced

2 red Thai chilies, thinly sliced

1 cup (250 mL) finely chopped flat-leaf parsley

1 Tbsp (15 mL) fresh thyme leaves

1 lemon, juiced and zested

½ cup (125 mL) Panko breadcrumbs

1 small bunch cilantro, leaves only

STEAMED & BROILED RAZOR CLAMS

In this recipe, the razor clams take on the classic Oysters Rockefeller dish. Oysters Rockefeller is a staple dish I order any time I travel to New York City. The last time I was there, I had lunch at one of my favorite restaurants, an NYC landmark called Grand Central Oyster Bar. As always, I had my prized Rockefellers and a couple of craft beers, and then walked through the gourmet food market that's located in the station nearby. In the market, there is a great seafood section with tons of beautiful, sustainable seafood, and that's when I saw the razor clams and thought . . . *Hmmm, let's play with this pairing!* And here we are. I hope you enjoy it!

1. Rinse the clams under cold, running water and pull off any hair to debeard them. Dry the clams in a clean dish towel before proceeding. 2. In a large saucepan, heat 2 Tbsp (30 mL) of the olive oil over high heat. Once the oil is hot—it will shimmer in the pan—add the razor clams, still in their shells, and wine, and cover. Steam the clams for 2 to 3 minutes, or until they've all opened. Discard any clams that do not open. Take the pan off the heat and remove the clams, reserving the liquid in the saucepan. Place the clams in a bowl until needed. 3. Turn down the heat to medium and then place the saucepan with the juices back on the stove. Add the remaining 2 Tbsp (30 mL) olive oil with the green onions, garlic, and chilies. Simmer for 2 to 3 minutes, or until the onions and garlic have softened slightly. Remove the pan from the heat and stir in the parsley, thyme, and lemon juice and zest (reserving a little bit of zest for garnish). Transfer the mixture to a bowl and let it cool. 4. Preheat the oven's broiler setting to high, with the rack at the highest position. 5. Cut the razor clams lengthwise to open them completely. Be sure to use your thumb to remove any of the digestive tract (dark color) that may be visible, but keep the meat inside the bottom shell. Spoon some green onion mixture into each razor clam, top with breadcrumbs, and then place the clams on a baking tray. 6. Place the tray of clams under the broiler for 2 to 3 minutes, or until the clams are golden brown. 7. Transfer the clams to a serving dish. Garnish with the cilantro and lemon zest before serving.

Lunch

SERVES 4–6

2 lb (900 g) live littleneck clams

2 Tbsp (30 mL) unsalted butter

6 cloves garlic, minced

1 large shallot, finely diced

Kosher salt and freshly ground black pepper

1 cup (250 mL) orange juice, freshly squeezed

¼ cup (60 mL) fresh mint, chopped then measured

¾ cup (175 mL) unsalted butter, melted, for dipping

French baguette, for serving

STEAMERS! EAST COAST CLASSIC

This recipe is an East Coast staple that has been passed down from generation to generation in my family, but everyone has a slightly different way of making it. The main reason I love dishes like this one is that they're perfect to share with your loved ones. I remember as a kid going on our East Coast family road trips and eating several of these steamed clams at restaurants along the way.

1. Rinse the clams under cold, running water and pull off any hair to debeard them. **2.** Heat a large sauté pan over medium heat. Once hot, add the butter, and allow it to melt. Add the garlic and shallots and salt and pepper, to taste. Cook for 2 to 3 minutes, or until soft and fragrant. Add the orange juice and simmer, uncovered, for approximately 2 minutes. Add the clams to the pan, stirring well. Cover the pan with a tight-fitting lid and steam the clams for 8 to 10 minutes, or until they've all opened. Using a slotted spoon, remove the clams from the cooking broth and discard any that did not open. **3.** Divide the hot broth and steamed clams evenly between serving bowls. Garnish with the fresh mint and dip each clam into warm melted butter. Use pieces of the baguette to sop up the broth.

CRAB

Party!

CHILLED KING CRAB LEGS & MATTY'S SEAFOOD COCKTAIL SAUCE

SERVES 4–6

6 frozen pre-cooked Alaskan king crab legs, thawed

4 sprigs fresh tarragon

2 lemons, quartered

Matty's Seafood Cocktail Sauce, for dipping (page 225)

I know everyone likely thinks that lobster is my favorite type of shellfish to eat, but I must come clean: chilled king crab is, hands-down, my absolute fave! It's also an ideal dish for any cocktail party because it's so easy to prepare. To make life simple, purchase frozen king crab legs, and remember to cut the pieces nice and small so your guests can eat them easily. Be careful cracking these crab clusters, as their spikes are extremely sharp. This recipe can easily be doubled for larger gatherings.

1. Using kitchen shears, cut from the bottom of the crab leg to the top, or to the highest point you can reach, and then turn the shell over and cut back down to the bottom of the shell. Remove the piece of cut crab shell to expose the meat, but leave the meat inside the shell. Repeat with all the legs. Place the crab legs on a serving platter. 2. Chiffonade the fresh tarragon by stacking the leaves, rolling them up into a bunch, and then thinly slicing the leaves perpendicular to the roll.
3. Garnish the crab legs with the tarragon chiffonade and a squeeze of lemon juice. Arrange the remaining lemon quarters around the edge of the serving platter and serve with a dish of Matty's Seafood Cocktail Sauce.

Dinner

SERVES 4–6

3 lb (1.3 kg) frozen king crab
legs, thawed

1 Tbsp (15 mL) unsalted butter

2 Tbsp (30 mL) minced garlic

1 cup (250 mL) fish stock

1 tsp (5 mL) kosher salt

1 tsp (5 mL) freshly ground
black pepper

Clarified butter, for dipping
(page 224)

NOTE: *Add an orange, lime,
lemon, and bay leaf to the
saucepan during steaming for
a fresh, citrus flavor.*

STEAMED KING CRAB

Each time I make this dish, it reminds me to respect the fishermen and their families who are in the line of work of catching live king crabs, as it's far from easy. They deal with some of the harshest weather conditions around.

1. Using kitchen shears, cut the top sections of the crab legs into large pieces.
2. In a large skillet, melt the butter over medium heat. Add the garlic and cook for approximately 1 minute. Do not let it burn. Add the crab leg pieces (in their shells), fish stock, salt, and pepper. Stir well to combine. Cover the skillet and steam the crab leg pieces for 3 to 5 minutes, or until the stock has almost reduced completely. If there's too much crab to fit in your skillet without crowding, divide the butter, garlic, and stock in two, and repeat the process in batches. 3. Serve hot with clarified butter for dipping.

Dinner

INDIAN CURRY CRAB

SERVES 4

3 lb (1.3 kg) live blue crabs

1 large Roma tomato, finely chopped

½ white onion, diced

1 Tbsp (15 mL) canola oil

¼ cup (60 mL) minced garlic cloves

¼ cup (60 mL) diced shallots

¼ cup (60 mL) finely diced fresh ginger

¼ cup (60 mL) green chili paste

1 tsp (5 mL) curry powder

1 tsp (5 mL) ground turmeric

1 tsp (5 mL) chili powder

1 tsp (5 mL) ground coriander

½ cup (125 mL) canned or fresh tomato purée (see note)

Kosher salt, to taste

Cilantro, for garnish

This rich, creamy yellow curry must be one of the most fragrant recipes I make. The beautiful aroma of this dish will fill your kitchen and instantly take you to a faraway land. One of the reasons I love living in Toronto, Canada, is that it's so multicultural. There are incredible restaurants in this beautiful city, and some of my personal favorites specialize in Indian cuisine. This dish was inspired by all the complex and flavorful meals I've eaten in this city!

1. In a large saucepan with a steamer insert, bring 4 cups (1 L) of cold water to a boil over high heat and place the crabs in the freezer for 20 minutes to put them into a catatonic state. Carefully place the steamer insert into the saucepan, letting it settle above the water line. Transfer the crabs to the pan, and steam, covered, for 20 to 25 minutes, or until the crabs turn a bright orange-red. Remove the saucepan from the heat and, using tongs, remove the crabs one at a time from the steamer and place them on a cutting board. Using a sharp kitchen knife, remove the shells from the back of the crabs and discard them. Remove all the intestinal parts. Cut the shells in half or quarters so they'll all take the same length of time to cook. Set aside in the fridge. 2. In a food processor fitted with the steel blade, blend the tomatoes and onions together. Set aside. 3. In a large skillet, heat the oil over medium heat for 30 seconds to 1 minute, or until it starts to shimmer. Add the garlic and shallots, and sauté for a few minutes until they become soft and translucent. Add the tomato and onion mixture, and sauté for an additional 2 to 3 minutes, stirring occasionally. 4. Turn down the heat to low and then add the ginger and green chili paste. Continue to cook for another 1 to 2 minutes, stirring constantly. Add the curry powder, turmeric, chili powder, and coriander and give it all a good stir. Add the tomato purée, mix to combine, and cook for another minute or so. Add 1 cup (250 mL) cold water, bring to a boil, and reduce to a simmer for another 5 to 7 minutes. Add the crabs, stir well, and cook for 3 to 5 minutes, or until the crab meat is hot. 5. Dish the curry immediately into bowls and garnish with cilantro. A side of rice is always delicious with this dish.

NOTE: If you'd prefer to use homemade tomato purée for this recipe, cook about ½ lb (225 g) of on-the-vine tomatoes in boiling water over high heat for 8 to 12 minutes, or until soft. Remove the tomatoes from the saucepan and then carefully peel off and discard the skins. In a food processor fitted with the steel blade, blend the tomatoes until smooth and then run the mixture through a fine-mesh sieve to remove the seeds, pressing down with a wooden spoon to extract as much flesh as you can. Place the purée in the saucepan and heat on low, stirring, until the mixture has reduced to a paste.

Party!

SERVES 6–8

2 lemons, cut in half

4 Tbsp (60 mL) seafood
seasoning, divided, plus
more for garnish

1 Tbsp (15 mL) kosher salt

3 lb (1.3 kg) live blue crabs

10 small new potatoes,
quartered

6 ears of corn, cut in half

1 lb (450 g) your favorite
sausages, cut into 1-inch
(2.5 cm) rounds

2 cups (500 mL) baby arugula

2 cups (500 mL) unsalted
butter, melted

LOUISIANA CRAB BOIL

This recipe is simple and fun for the entire family, especially during the summer months. I've been to New Orleans, one of my favorite cities in the United States, twice and I can't wait to go back. The food, the people, the music, and the culture—it's all so cool. I urge you to go as soon as you can, if you haven't already been. To make this dining experience authentic, make sure to grab lots of newspapers and spread them out on a picnic or other large table. Grab a small wooden mallet, bibs, and hot drawn butter for dipping. This meal gets messy, but it's so worth it. Crack a few cold ones and enjoy!

1. In a very large saucepan over high heat, combine 8 cups (2 L) cold water with the lemons, 2 Tbsp (30 mL) of the seafood seasoning, and the salt. While it comes to a boil, place the crabs in the freezer for 20 minutes to put them into a catatonic state. Add the potatoes and corn to the saucepan and cook for 12 to 15 minutes, or until the potatoes are soft and the corn is cooked through. **2.** Turn down the heat to medium and then add the whole crabs, sausages, and remaining 2 Tbsp (30 mL) of seafood seasoning. Cook for 5 to 7 minutes, or until the crab is bright orange-red and the sausages are cooked through. Poke the sausages with the tip of a knife to ensure that the juices run clear, or use a meat thermometer to check their temperature. **3.** Drain and discard the water from the saucepan. **4.** Place a large serving platter or newspapers on a clean table. Pour the crabs and vegetables right on top. Garnish with baby arugula and more seafood seasoning, if desired. **5.** Grab that hot melted butter, dip, and enjoy!

MATTY'S SPICY CRAB & WHITE RICE

SERVES 2

1 large live mud or Dungeness crab (about 1 lb/450 g)

¼ tsp (1 mL) corn flour

1 cup (250 mL) white rice

1 Tbsp (15 mL) canola oil

2 yellow onions, roughly chopped

4 red Thai chilies, thinly sliced

½ cup (125 mL) canned or fresh tomato purée (page 44)

¼ cup (60 mL) soy sauce

¼ cup (60 mL) granulated sugar

2 tsp (10 mL) white vinegar

½ tsp (2 mL) kosher salt

Cilantro, for garnish

When I was traveling through Thailand, I noticed that this was a common recipe from restaurant to restaurant. It always featured mud crabs, which are specific to southeast Asia. If you can't find mud crabs, use Dungeness crabs. Remember: you need patience, patience, patience when you're cooking with any fragrant spices and sauces.

1. In a large saucepan, bring 4 cups (1 L) salted water to a boil over high heat and place the crab in the freezer for 20 minutes to put it into a catatonic state. Transfer the crab to the saucepan and cook for 4 to 6 minutes to parboil. The crab will be bright red. Using tongs, carefully remove the crab from the boiling water. Discard the water. 2. Once the crab is cool enough to handle, remove the top shell and chop the crab into quarters (keep the meat in the shell). Using the flat of a large knife, crack the claws to allow the flavors to infuse into the meat and shell. 3. In a small mixing bowl, whisk the corn flour with ¼ cup (60 mL) cold water. Set aside at room temperature. 4. In a separate large saucepan, bring 2 cups (500 mL) of salted water to a boil over high heat. Add the rice and stir. Cover the saucepan with a lid and turn down the temperature to a simmer, allowing the rice to cook for 18 to 20 minutes, or until light and fluffy. 5. Meanwhile, in a wok, heat the canola oil over medium-high heat until it shimmers. Add the onions, chilies, tomato purée, soy sauce, sugar, vinegar, and salt. Mix thoroughly and then sauté for 2 to 3 minutes, just until the onions begin to soften. Add the corn flour mixture, stir well, and bring everything to a simmer. 6. Turn down the wok's heat to medium and add the crab pieces. Cook for 8 to 10 minutes, turning the crab pieces occasionally, or until the shells of the crab are heated through. 7. Divide the crab mixture between two serving bowls and garnish with cilantro. Serve with the rice.

Dinner

SERVES 2

1 large live Dungeness crab
(about 1 lb/450 g)

1 cup (250 mL) white rice

2 tsp (10 mL) canola oil

1 Tbsp (15 mL) soy sauce

1 Tbsp (15 mL) brown sugar

1 tsp (5 mL) yellow curry
powder

1 tsp (5 mL) minced garlic

½ cup (125 mL) chicken stock

1 large egg, beaten

1 can (13 ½ oz/400 mL)
coconut milk, full-fat

2 stalks Chinese celery, cut
into large dice (found at
Asian markets)

1 red Thai chili

1 bunch cilantro, leaves only,
for garnish

PHUKET THAI CURRY CRAB

Visiting Thailand for the first time was a life-altering experience; it made me view the world in a completely different way. I thought the entire country was incredible, from the big city hustle of Bangkok to the beauty of the beaches on the southern islands. One of my most memorable experiences was learning to make this delicious centuries-old crab recipe. If you're ever in Phuket, go visit my buddy Jon, who owns the Crab House, and tell him MDP sent you. You'll be treated like family!

1. Place the crab in the freezer for 20 minutes to put it into a catatonic state. Then remove the top portion of the shell from the crab by lifting it from the body section—it should come off easily. Use a good knife to chop the body portion into large pieces. As best you can, remove the crab meat from the body pieces and place the lump meat into a bowl, discarding all bits of shell. Crack the claws and legs by hitting them with the flat of the knife. Using your fingers or a pick, remove the crab meat from the claws and legs and add it to the bowl. Set the meat aside at room temperature, and discard the body and all shell pieces. **2.** In a saucepan, bring 2 cups (500 mL) of salted water to a boil over high heat. Stir in the rice. Cover the saucepan with a lid and turn down the heat to a simmer, allowing the rice to cook for 18 to 20 minutes, or until light and fluffy. **3.** In a wok over low heat, warm the canola oil. Once the oil starts to shimmer, add the soy sauce, sugar, and curry powder. Cook, stirring constantly, for 30 seconds to combine the flavors. Add the garlic and cook, stirring occasionally, for 2 to 3 minutes, or until light brown and fragrant. Add the crab meat and stir-fry for 3 to 5 minutes, or until cooked through. Pour in the chicken stock and mix well. Add the egg, stir well, and cook for 1 to 2 minutes, or until the egg is completely cooked. Add the coconut milk, Chinese celery, and Thai chili. Stir well and then cook for 2 to 3 minutes, or until the coconut milk has slightly reduced and the mixture has taken on the look of a sauce—it should coat the back of a spoon. **4.** Divide the curry between two serving bowls and garnish with cilantro. Serve with the rice.

Lunch

SERVES 2

1 cup (250 mL) freshly cooked or canned snow crab meat (see note)

¼ cup (60 mL) full-fat mayonnaise

Juice and zest of 1 lemon

1 tsp (5 mL) Dijon mustard

1 tsp (5 mL) chili powder

1 small iceberg lettuce, leaves separated

SNOW CRAB LETTUCE CUPS

Okay, here's what I like to call a win-win recipe because it's both simple to make and healthy for you! I love the crisp texture of the lettuce, the pop of spice in the mustard, and the sweetness of the crab. I'll sometimes use canned or packaged crab meat to help speed up the preparation time.

1. In a medium-size bowl, combine the crab meat, mayonnaise, lemon juice, mustard, and chili powder. Stir well. Cover and refrigerate until ready to serve.

2. To serve, arrange a lettuce leaf to form a cup and pile the crab mixture in the middle. Top with a sprinkle of lemon zest and wrap the lettuce around the crab. Repeat with the remaining ingredients.

NOTES: If you're looking to raise the visual appeal of the dish for your guests, top the lettuce cups with edible flowers. Try substituting Sriracha hot sauce for the Dijon mustard to add a spicier spin to it.
  If you're using freshly cooked snow crab, you'll need a 2 lb (900 g) crab to produce 1 cup (250 mL) of meat.

※

You can buy pre-cooked snow crab meat in most grocery stores. It makes this recipe perfect for a busy weekday lunch.

SERVES 2–4

4 live soft-shell crabs (about ¼ lb/110 g each)

½ cup (125 mL) all-purpose flour

1 tsp (5 mL) cayenne pepper

1 tsp (5 mL) seasoned salt

1 Tbsp (15 mL) canola oil

Kosher salt

1 lemon, quartered

TEX MEX SPICY SOFT-SHELL CRAB

Soft-shell crabs are perfect for this recipe as the sweetness of the crabs balances out the spiciness of the cayenne pepper. To turn up the spice level on this dish, simply add chili flakes and fresh jalapeño pepper to the crab while it's cooking.

1. Place the crabs in the freezer for 20 minutes to put them into a catatonic state. Using kitchen shears, cut the face off one crab, right behind the eyes. This will kill it instantly. You're only cutting about ½-inch (1.2 cm) off. Flip the crab over to the bottom side and pull up on the middle latch-type piece, known as the apron. Cut it right off the crab and discard it. Turn the crab back over, lift off the shell, discard it, and remove any other pieces that are not clearly meat. Repeat this process with the remaining crabs. Rinse the crabs under cold water and set aside for a few minutes. 2. In a small dish, mix together the flour, cayenne pepper, and seasoned salt. Lightly coat the crab meat in the flour. 3. In a large skillet, heat the canola oil over medium-high heat. Line a plate with paper towels. 4. When the oil is hot, add two of the crabs and cook for 3 to 4 minutes per side. Remove the cooked crabs from the skillet and place them on the prepared plate to absorb any excess oil. Sprinkle with a pinch of salt. Repeat with the two remaining crabs. 5. Serve the crabs hot or at room temperature, with the lemon quarters.

Party!

SERVES 4–6

Tater Tots

2 lb (900 g) Yukon Gold potatoes

¾ cup (175 mL) full-fat sour cream

1 cup (250 mL) shredded aged
white cheddar cheese

2 Tbsp (30 mL) finely chopped chives

2 Tbsp (30 mL) finely diced red Thai chilies

1 cup (250 mL) freshly cooked or canned
snow crab meat (see note on p 50)

1 cup (250 mL) all-purpose flour

1 large egg, beaten

1 cup (250 mL) Panko breadcrumbs

4 cups (1 L) canola oil

Kosher salt and freshly ground black pepper

Cheese Sauce

1 tsp (5 mL) canola oil

1 shallot, finely diced

2 Tbsp (30 mL) unsalted butter

2 Tbsp (30 mL) all-purpose flour

1 cup (250 mL) 2% milk

1 Tbsp (15 mL) cayenne pepper

½ cup (125 mL) aged cheddar cheese, grated

½ cup (125 mL) grated Gouda cheese

SNOW CRAB TATER TOTS

This fun recipe is one of my all-time favorite snacks. I especially love making it around the Christmas holidays, as it seems to bring cheer to my entire family. It combines tater tots, one of the most classic comfort foods, and sweet, delicious snow crab. These light and fluffy little pillows of crab and potato will be the big hit at your next party, and this recipe can easily be doubled for larger gatherings.

1. Preheat the oven to 375°F (190°C). **2.** For the tater tots, scrub the potatoes and then wrap them in aluminum foil. Using a fork, stab each one all over 10 to 15 times. Place them on a baking tray and bake for 20 to 25 minutes, or until they're soft enough to pierce with a fork. You're not looking to fully cook the potatoes here, since you fry them later. Rotate the tray halfway through to ensure even cooking. **3.** Allow the potatoes to cool enough to handle, slice in half lengthwise, and scoop out the flesh. **4.** In a large mixing bowl, combine the baked potato flesh with the sour cream, cheddar, chives, and Thai chilies. Mix well to break up the flesh of the potato. Add the crab meat to the potato mixture and stir to combine. Set aside in the fridge. **5.** Set up a dredging station by placing the flour, beaten egg, and breadcrumbs in three separate shallow bowls. Line a baking tray with parchment paper. **6.** Using your hands, shape the potato mixture into 1 ½-inch-long (4 cm) cylinders. Gently roll this cylinder in the flour, dip it in the egg, and then dip it in the breadcrumbs. Gently shake it to remove any excess breadcrumbs. Repeat with the remaining potato mixture. Place the coated cylinders on the prepared baking tray. Cover the tots with plastic wrap and refrigerate for 2 to 3 hours to set, so they're easier to fry. **7.** In a deep saucepan, heat the canola oil to 350°F (180°C). Use a cooking thermometer to check the temperature. **8.** Preheat the oven to 200°F (93°C). Line an ovenproof plate with paper towels. **9.** Using tongs, place the tots, in small batches to avoid overcrowding the pan, in the hot oil for 1 to 2 minutes, or until they float and are golden brown. If the temperature of the oil drops, bring it back up before starting the next batch. Using tongs again, lift the fried tots from the hot oil to the prepared plate, season with salt and pepper to taste, cover with aluminum foil, and place in the oven to keep warm until you're ready to eat. They can stay in the oven for about 30 minutes before drying out. If you're going to serve them past that time, turn off the oven and just warm them through again before serving. **10.** For the cheese sauce, in a small saucepan over medium heat, warm the canola oil. Add the shallots and cook for 2 to 3 minutes, or until translucent. Add the butter, letting it melt and turn bubbly and brown. Whisk in the flour and then slowly whisk the mixture until it becomes a paste. Turn down the heat to low and then add the milk and cayenne pepper. Cook for 3 to 4 minutes, or until the milk starts to reduce in volume. Add both cheeses, whisking well until velvety and smooth in texture. Remove from the heat and transfer the sauce to a small bowl. **11.** Serve the tots nice and hot, dipped in the cheese sauce.

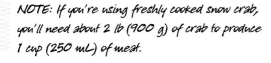

NOTE: If you're using freshly cooked snow crab, you'll need about 2 lb (900 g) of crab to produce 1 cup (250 mL) of meat.

Brunch

SERVES 2–4

2 large zucchinis

2 Tbsp (30 mL) canola oil

1 medium semi-firm avocado

½ cup (125 mL) red pepper
hummus

¾ cup (175 mL) freshly
cooked or canned cooked
snow crab meat

2 red Thai chilies, finely diced

½ medium red onion, finely
diced

Hot sauce, for serving

SNOW CRAB ZUCCHINI ROLLS

These rolls are a fun take on pinwheels. I love innovation in the kitchen. After all, without creativity, we would just cook and eat the same thing over and over again. One of my very favorite kitchen tools is the mandolin. With a little practice it can take your cooking and presentation of dishes to the next level!

1. Using a mandolin or vegetable peeler, thinly slice the zucchinis into six to eight long strips. 2. In a nonstick sauté pan over medium-high heat, warm the canola oil. Add the zucchini strips, without overlapping (do this in batches, if necessary), and cook for 30 to 60 seconds per side, or until slightly cooked and soft. Transfer the zucchini slices to a plate, cover loosely with plastic wrap, and place in the refrigerator until needed. 3. Cut the avocado into ¼-inch (6 mm) cubes and set aside. 4. Lay the thin slices of zucchini out flat on a working surface. Spread one side of each strip with hummus and add a layer of crab meat, avocado cubes, chilies, and onions. Starting from one end, slowly roll the zucchini strips, tightly folding in the crab mixture. You can close this with a toothpick, or just leave the end tucked underneath. 5. Serve cold with your favorite hot sauce.

NOTES: You can also serve this dish hot. Simply place the finished rolls in a 375°F (190°C) oven for 3 to 5 minutes, or until warm throughout. If you're using freshly cooked snow crab, you'll need about 1 ½ lb (680 g) of crab to produce ¾ cup (175 mL) of meat.

EXOTIC SHELLFISH

Dinner

SERVES 2–4

1–2 large queen conch (1 cup/250 mL meat)

¼ cup (60 mL) kosher salt

Juice from 4 limes

¼ cup (60 mL) mango juice

¼ cup (60 mL) coconut water

1 small Roma tomato, diced

½ small red onion, diced

1 tsp (5 mL) ground cinnamon

Kosher salt and freshly ground black pepper

1 Tbsp (15 mL) unsweetened shredded coconut, toasted, for garnish

Tortilla chips, for serving

BAHAMA MAMA FARMED QUEEN CONCH CEVICHE

I should have named this recipe Sky Juice Ceviche! Sky Juice is the Bahamian national drink. People sell it from roadside stands and in restaurants. It's made of coconut milk, coconut water, and spices. And I think it's the perfect base for this conch dish. It's important to note that wild conch has been overfished and should currently be avoided. The best alternative is to buy farmed queen conch, which has become popular in recent years.

1. Rinse the conch shell under cold, running water and then wrap it in a dish towel. Using a large fork, pull the meat out. If this proves difficult, carefully hit the shell with a large hammer or mallet. Remove the meat from the shell and rinse it to remove any shell pieces. Fresh conch meat is tough, so place it in a bowl with the ¼ cup (60 mL) of salt and enough cold water to completely cover it for 2 to 3 hours. This will help break down and tenderize the meat. If the meat is still tough after soaking in the water, use a meat tenderizer to hit it until it's soft. **2.** Once the meat is tender, roughly chop it. **3.** In a large mixing bowl, combine the conch meat and lime juice. Cover and refrigerate for minimum 1 ½ to maximum 2 ½ hours. **4.** Remove the bowl from the refrigerator. Add the mango juice, coconut water, tomatoes, onions, cinnamon, and salt and pepper to taste. Mix well to combine the flavors. **5.** Spoon the ceviche into a serving bowl. Garnish with the toasted shredded coconut and serve with tortilla chips.

FARMED QUEEN CONCH SHACK FRITTERS

SERVES 2–4

2 cups + 2 tsp (510 mL) canola oil, divided

2 ears of corn, kernels removed

1 small Yukon Gold or white potato, shredded

1 large red bell pepper, diced

1 clove garlic, finely diced

1 cup (250 mL) finely chopped conch meat (about 1–2 large queen conch)

2 cups (500 mL) all-purpose flour

1 tsp (5 mL) ground allspice

2 large eggs, beaten

1 cup (250 mL) buttermilk

Sriracha Mayo (page 226), for serving

Ponzu Sauce (page 226), for serving

There's no better choice in the Bahamas than conch fritters! My fiancée, Dana, and I loved eating these while vacationing there a few years ago. At times I felt like I was in a James Bond movie with the scenery: ocean, casinos, and massive yachts. My life doesn't often resemble a James Bond movie, but this dish reminds me of those moments. This recipe can easily be doubled for a larger gathering.

1. In a large skillet, heat 2 tsp (10 mL) of canola oil over medium-high heat. Add the corn kernels, potatoes, bell peppers, and garlic. Cook for 2 to 3 minutes, or until soft, stirring occasionally. Add the conch meat, mix to combine, and cook for an additional 1 to 2 minutes, or until the meat is warmed through. Remove the skillet from the heat and allow the mixture to cool completely. 2. In a large mixing bowl, mix the flour and allspice with the eggs and buttermilk. Add the cooled conch mixture and mix again. 3. In a large cast iron skillet, heat the remaining 2 cups (500 mL) of canola oil over high heat until it shimmers. You'll need enough to completely cover the fritters. Line a plate with paper towels and preheat your oven to 200°F (93°C). 4. To fry the fritters, place 1 Tbsp (15 mL) of the conch batter mixture in the hot oil, working with 1 to 2 fritters at a time. Cook for 2 to 3 minutes, flipping once, or until they float to the surface and are golden brown. Using a metal slotted spoon, remove the fritters from the oil and transfer to the prepared plate to absorb any excess oil. Transfer the cooked fritters to a baking tray and keep warm in the oven while you finish frying. 5. To serve, arrange the fritters on a plate with Sriracha Mayo and Ponzu Sauce for dipping.

Quick & Easy

SERVES 2–4

1 lb (450 g) periwinkles

2 Tbsp (30 mL) unsalted butter

2 cloves garlic, finely diced

1 leek, white part only, finely sliced

1 medium carrot, peeled and diced

1 stalk celery, diced

1 tsp (5 mL) chili flakes

1 cup (250 mL) dry white wine

¼ cup (60 mL) heavy (35%) cream

Kosher salt and freshly ground black pepper

2 Tbsp (30 mL) roughly chopped fresh flat-leaf parsley, for garnish

PARISIAN PERIWINKLES

This dish takes me back to Paris and some of the best dining experiences of my life. The first time I went there was 2006 and—*ooh là là!*—the classic French ingredients of butter, wine, heavy cream, and leeks were beyond delicious. But I have to admit, I couldn't quite pull off the sophistication of French dining culture. I remember eating periwinkles and spilling half the bowl on my lap. All I could do was laugh it off and order a glass of wine. Hopefully you have better luck than I had. *Bon appétit!*

1. Fill a large container with cool water. Place the periwinkles in the water, making sure they're completely covered, and let them sit for 30 to 45 minutes. This will rinse them out and clean them of any sand. Then, using a needle or small pick, gently poke each one. If they move, they're good for cooking and then eating. Discard any that don't move. 2. In a medium-size saucepan, bring 4 cups (1 L) of cold water to a boil over high heat. Add the periwinkles and par-cook them for 3 to 4 minutes. Using a slotted spoon, remove the periwinkles from the water and set them aside at room temperature. 3. In a large skillet, melt the butter over medium-high heat. Add the garlic, leeks, carrots, celery, and chili flakes. Cook for 2 to 3 minutes, or until soft and fragrant, stirring occasionally. Add the white wine and stir well. Add the heavy cream and continue to stir. Add the par-cooked periwinkles, cover, and cook for 2 more minutes. Season with salt and pepper to taste. 4. Spoon the periwinkles into a large serving bowl. Garnish with parsley and serve with toothpicks to help remove the meat from the shells.

Party!

SERVES 4–6

¾ cup (185 mL) seafood seasoning, divided

4 medium lemons, halved

2 lb (900 g) red potatoes, quartered

2 lb (900 g) spicy sausage, cut into 1-inch (2.5 cm) rounds

6 ears of corn, cut in half

10 lb (4.5 kg) live or frozen (thawed) crawfish

2 cups (500 mL) unsalted butter, melted

THE SAILORS' N'AWLINS CRAWFISH BOIL

Here it is, folks, another great recipe for eating with your hands. I think you know by now that I love that messy style of eating. I like to host crawfish dinners at home during the summer, and this Louisiana staple is perfect for any outdoor party. If you buy live crawfish, which may be tough to do unless you live in the southern United States, you'll need to clean or "purge" the crawfish before eating them (see the note, below). This recipe can easily be doubled for a larger gathering.

1. In a very large stockpot, bring 10 ½ quarts (10 L) of cold water to a boil over high heat. Add ½ cup (125 mL) of the seafood seasoning, the lemon halves, and the potato quarters. Bring the water back up to a boil and then cook for 8 to 10 minutes, or until the potatoes have softened slightly. Add the sausages and corn. Cook for 10 more minutes. Add the crawfish and cook for an additional 5 minutes. 2. Drain off the water, and allow the seafood to cool for 3 to 5 minutes, until cool enough to handle. 3. In the meantime, set up your serving table with a plastic tablecloth and plenty of newspapers. Pour the seafood right on the table. Sprinkle the remaining ¼ cup (60 mL) of seafood seasoning overtop. 4. Break out the napkins and cold beer, and dip the pieces into the melted butter. Don't worry about getting your hands dirty; it's all part of the fun!

NOTE: Purging is a simple process. Dump the live crawfish into a large cooler or stockpot. Empty one large box of kosher salt over the crawfish, and then add enough cold water to cover them all. Using a large spoon, stir well and allow the salt to clean out any mud or dirt. Let them soak for about 5 minutes and then drain off the water. The crawfish are now ready to cook. Remember to discard any dead or unmoving crawfish prior to cooking!

Dinner

SERVES 2–4

1 live sea urchin

2 cups (500 mL) dried penne
   pasta

4 slices of baguette, cut about
   ¼-inch (6 mm) thick

¼ cup (75 mL) extra-virgin
   olive oil

1 Tbsp (15 mL) unsalted butter

½ cup (125 mL) 2% milk

1 Tbsp (15 mL) all-purpose
   flour

Kosher salt and freshly ground
   black pepper

SEA URCHIN CROSTINI & PENNE PASTA

During my recent trip to Japan, I fell in love with sea urchins because the ways to prepare them seem endless. Also known as uni, they're mostly famously prepared raw for sushi. I absolutely love uni. But most of all, I like how even just a little bit of uni can add a fresh, sweet flavor to any dish. Grab some chilled sake and have some fun.

1. Preheat the oven to 400°F (200°C). 2. To open and clean the sea urchin, use kitchen scissors to cut back as many "quills" (the spikes) near the mouth opening as possible. Once you can access the mouth area, carefully place a knife in the mouth and crack the shell in half, exposing the inside of the urchin. Scoop away everything except the orange segments, which are the uni. Gently wash the opened half shells with the uni inside under cold, running water. Remove two pieces of uni, setting them aside in the fridge for the toast, and set the rest of the sea urchin aside in the fridge until needed. 3. Bring a large saucepan of salted water to a boil over medium-high heat. Add the pasta and cook until al dente. Drain the pasta, but reserve ¼ cup (60 mL) of the pasta water in case the sauce is too thick and you need to thin it out. 4. Drizzle the baguette slices with the olive oil and place them on a baking tray. Bake for 2 to 3 minutes, or until crispy and turning golden brown. Remove the crostini from the oven and set aside. 5. In a medium-size saucepan, melt the butter over medium-high heat. Add the milk and then whisk in the flour. Turn down the heat to low. Slowly whisk to remove any lumps. Add the remaining uni pieces and then increase the heat to medium. Whisk to break up the uni into the sauce. Season to taste with salt and pepper. 6. Add the pasta to the sauce and mix well to coat. 7. In a small mixing bowl, mash the two reserved piece of uni with a fork until smooth. Spoon the mixture onto the baguette slices. 8. Serve the pasta in bowls with the sea urchin crostini on the side.

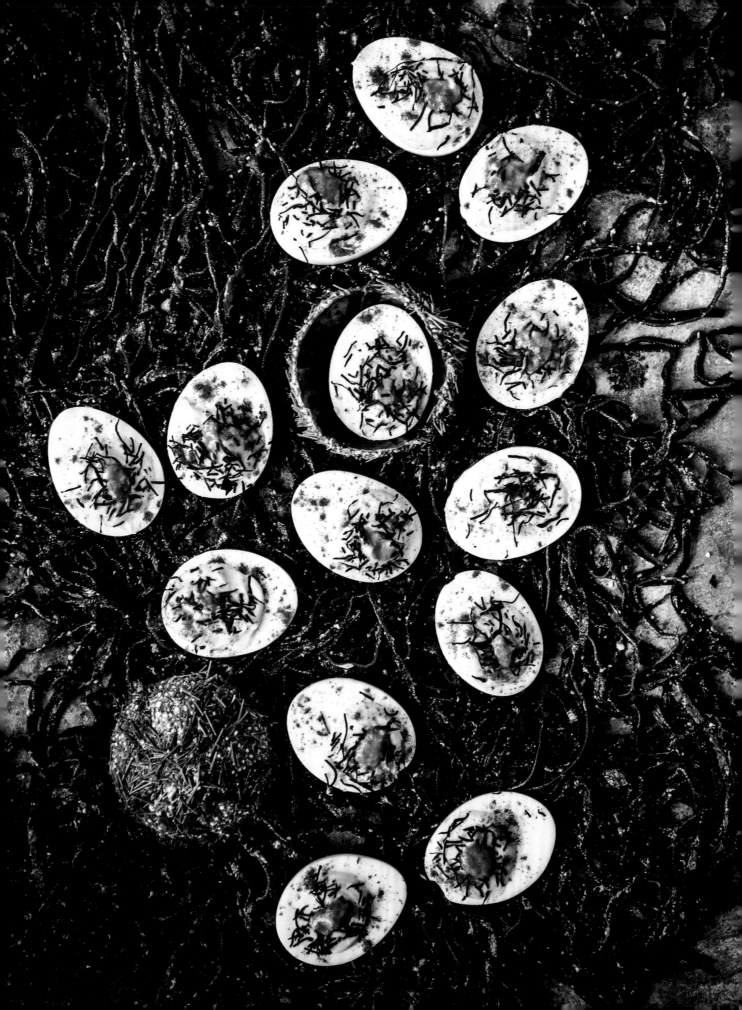

Party!

SERVES 12

1 live sea urchin

12 large eggs, hardboiled, shells removed, and cut in half lengthwise

½ cup (125 mL) full-fat mayonnaise

Juice from 1 lemon

2 tsp (10 mL) rice wine vinegar

Kosher salt and freshly ground black pepper

1 Tbsp (15 mL) smoked paprika

2 Tbsp (30 mL) dried seaweed, ground into dust (see note)

NOTE: *To grind the seaweed, or nori, into dust, you can use a mortar and pestle, or blitz it in your food processor.*

SEA URCHIN DEVILED EGGS

As a child, I loved eating deviled eggs. My memory is a little bit foggy, but I think it was my babysitter Elaine who would make these 1980s classics for me. The recipe below is certainly amped up from hers, but I don't think she'd mind. Hopefully you'll be impressed too!

1. To open and clean the sea urchin, use kitchen scissors to cut back as many "quills" (the spikes) near the mouth opening as possible. Once you can access the mouth area, carefully place a knife in the mouth and crack the shell in half, exposing the inside of the urchin. Scoop away everything except the orange segments, which are called uni. Gently wash the opened half shells with the uni inside under cold, running water. Remove two pieces of uni, setting them aside for the egg yolk mixture, and set the rest of the uni aside in the fridge for the garnish.
2. Carefully remove the egg yolks from the boiled eggs, keeping the whites intact, and place them in a mixing bowl. Place the egg white halves on a serving platter.
3. Add the two pieces of uni, the mayonnaise, lemon juice, rice wine vinegar, and salt and pepper to taste to the mixing bowl with the egg yolks. Using your hands, gently mix all the ingredients together until you get a smooth paste. 4. Scoop the egg mixture into a piping bag fitted with a star tip, and pipe the filling into the egg whites. Garnish each egg half with a pinch of paprika, seaweed dust, and reserved uni.

LOBSTER

LOBSTER & SHRIMP CEVICHE

SERVES 2–4

1 live lobster (1 ½ lb/680 g) or 2–3 frozen (thawed) lobster tails

½ lb (225 g) medium raw shrimp, weighed then peeled

1 medium red onion, thinly sliced

1 cup (250 mL) halved cherry tomatoes

½ English cucumber, sliced ¼-inch (6 mm) thick and finely chopped

½ cup (125 mL) finely chopped cilantro

Juice from 1 lemon

¼ cup (60 mL) fresh orange juice

Juice from 1 lime

1 Tbsp (15 mL) extra-virgin olive oil

Flaky sea salt and freshly ground black pepper

Tortilla chips or Bibb lettuce, for serving

The key to a great ceviche is to always use the freshest ingredients possible. I love how fresh seafood smells just like ocean air and the sea! When I traveled to Chile, I visited a town on the coast called Viña del Mar. It was there that I had the best ceviche I've ever tasted. It's been my goal to recreate that dish, and I think I'm very close!

1. If using live lobster, place it in the freezer for approximately 20 minutes to put it into a catatonic state. Using a sharp knife, pierce directly through the top of the lobster's head (this will kill it instantly) and run the knife down through the center of the lobster's body to split it into two. Using kitchen shears or a sharp knife, remove the meat and rinse it thoroughly under cold, running water. Finely chop the lobster meat. If using thawed, frozen lobster tails, remove the meat and finely chop it. 2. Roughly chop the shrimp. 3. In a large mixing bowl, mix together the lobster meat, shrimp, onions, tomatoes, cucumbers, cilantro, citrus juices, olive oil, and salt and pepper to taste to combine the flavors and allow the citrus to cook the meat. Cover the bowl tightly with aluminum foil or plastic wrap, and refrigerate for 1 ½ to 2 hours. The lobster and shrimp will be opaque and firm. 4. Remove the bowl from refrigerator and drain off any liquid. Serve the ceviche with tortilla chips, or use Bibb lettuce to make lettuce wraps.

Party!

SERVES 6–8

Cheese Balls

1 live lobster (1 ½ lb/680 g)

1 cup (250 mL) full-fat cream cheese

½ cup (125 mL) goat cheese

1 cup (250 mL) shredded aged cheddar cheese

1½ cups (375 mL) Italian breadcrumbs

1 cup (250 mL) all-purpose flour

2 large eggs

½ cup (125 mL) Panko breadcrumbs

3 cups (750 mL) canola oil (or more if required)

Kosher salt

8–12 basil leaves

½ cup (125 mL) grated Parmigiano-Reggiano cheese

Sauce

1 can (28 oz/796 mL) crushed tomatoes

4 Roma tomatoes, diced

6 basil leaves, minced

1 Tbsp (15 mL) olive oil

1 tsp (5 mL) onion powder

Kosher salt and freshly ground black pepper

ITALY MEETS EAST COAST FRIED LOBSTER CHEESE BALLS

These cheese balls were inspired by my time in Italy, and they make an awesome party platter appetizer! The rich flavors that come through in the zesty tomato sauce will improve any dish you make for the next week, so feel free to make a bit extra.

1. Prepare an ice bath in a bucket or the sink. 2. In a large saucepan over high heat, bring 12 cups (3 L) of salted, cold water to a boil. Using tongs, submerge the lobster, head first, in the boiling water, and cook, covered, for 8 to 10 minutes, or until the lobster turns bright red. Using tongs, transfer the lobster to the ice bath for 5 to 10 minutes to stop the cooking process. Then, using a large chef's knife or kitchen shears, carefully crack and break down the shell and remove as much meat as possible. Finely chop the meat and set it aside in the fridge. 3. To make the sauce, in a medium-size saucepan over medium-low heat, combine the canned and fresh tomatoes, basil, olive oil, onion powder, and salt and pepper to taste. Cook for 12 to 15 minutes, stirring occasionally, or until the sauce has thickened. Cover the saucepan, and keep it warm until needed. 4. In a large mixing bowl, mix the lobster meat with the cream cheese, goat cheese, and cheddar cheese. Add the Italian breadcrumbs and stir to combine. 5. Line a baking tray with parchment paper. 6. Using your hands, roll the lobster mixture into balls about 1 inch (2.5 cm) in diameter. Place the balls on the prepared baking tray, cover the tray with plastic wrap, and refrigerate for 2 to 3 hours to set. 7. Set up a dredging station by placing the flour in a small bowl, whisking the eggs in a second small bowl, and placing the Panko in a third bowl. Line a plate with paper towels. 8. Dredge each ball in the flour, and then roll in the egg wash, and then the Panko to coat evenly. Return to the baking tray. 9. Fill a large saucepan or home-use deep-fryer three-quarters full with the canola oil. Heat over medium-high heat until it reaches 350°F (180°C). 10. Using a metal slotted spoon, slowly add two to three balls at a time (don't overcrowd the pan) and fry them for approximately 2 minutes, or until they float and are golden brown. Using the slotted spoon, transfer the fried balls to the prepared plate to absorb any excess oil. Sprinkle with salt to taste. Let the oil come back up to temperature before proceeding with the next batch. 11. Chiffonade the basil by stacking the leaves, rolling them tightly, and then slicing them thinly perpendicular to the roll. 12. Spread some tomato sauce on each serving plate and top with three or four lobster cheese balls. Garnish with the Parmigiano-Reggiano cheese and basil chiffonade.

KOH TAO THAILAND LOBSTER PAD THAI

Dinner

SERVES 2–4

1 live lobster (1 ½ lb/680 g)

1 package (18 oz/500 g) dried vermicelli rice noodles

3 Tbsp (45 mL) peanut oil, divided

4 cloves garlic, diced

2 Tbsp (30 mL) minced fresh ginger

2 Tbsp (30 mL) brown sugar

2 Tbsp (30 mL) fish sauce

1 lemongrass stalk

Juice from 1 lemon

Juice from 1 lime

1 Tbsp (15 mL) ketchup

1 Tbsp (15 mL) Sriracha hot sauce

2 large eggs

2 Thai red chilies, thinly sliced

¼ cup (60 mL) crushed peanuts

¼ cup (60 mL) bean sprouts

¼ cup (60 mL) cilantro

It seems to me that really tasty, and sometimes unusual, street food can be found on every street in Thailand. During my travels there, I even saw grilled beetles and scorpions on sticks! But unless you've lost some sort of a bet, I suggest you stick to the more traditional street foods like this delicious Pad Thai. My favorite version of this dish came from the southern island of Koh Tao. I'm sure you'll love it too! The flavors are bold and the lobster is so sweet. A perfect combination.

1. Prepare an ice bath in a bucket or the sink. 2. To cook the lobster, in a large saucepan over high heat, bring 12 cups (3 L) of cold, salted water to a boil. Using tongs, submerge the lobster, head first, in the boiling water, and cook, covered, for 8 to 10 minutes, or until the lobster turns bright red. Using tongs again, remove the lobster from the water and place it in the ice bath for 5 to 10 minutes to stop the cooking process. Then, using a large chef's knife or kitchen shears, carefully crack and break down the shell and remove as much meat as possible. Roughly chop the meat and set aside in the fridge until needed. 3. In a medium-size saucepan over high heat, bring 4 cups (1 L) of cold water to a boil. Add the rice noodles and cook, stirring occasionally, for 1 to 2 minutes, or until soft. Drain the water from the saucepan and let the noodles sit in a sieve until needed. 4. In a large saucepan over medium-high heat, place 2 Tbsp (30 mL) of the peanut oil, and the garlic, ginger, sugar, and fish sauce. Stir well to combine. Turn down the heat to medium-low and cook for 2 to 3 minutes, or until fragrant. Stir occasionally. 5. To prepare the lemongrass stalk, remove the outer layers and bruise the remaining stalk with your chef's knife. Cut it into three or four pieces and add it to the sauce, along with the lobster meat and the lemon and lime juices. Stir well and then cook for 2 to 3 minutes, or until the flavors have infused the lobster meat. 6. Add the ketchup and hot sauce to the rice noodles. Mix well to evenly coat the rice noodles. Transfer the rice noodles to a large serving bowl and spoon the lobster meat mixture overtop. 7. In a small skillet, heat the remaining 1 Tbsp (15 mL) peanut oil and cook the eggs for approximately 2 minutes, or until the whites have set but aren't hard. Gently flip the eggs and cook for another 45 seconds to 1 minute. 8. Carefully garnish the serving bowl with the eggs, Thai chilies, crushed peanuts, bean sprouts, and cilantro. Serve family-style.

Lunch

LOBSTER BURRATA SALAD

SERVES 2-4

1 live lobster (1 ½ lb/680 g)

2 cups (500 mL) baby spinach

1 cup (250 mL) halved cherry tomatoes

1 Tbsp (15 mL) extra-virgin olive oil

1 tsp (5 mL) agave nectar

Flaky sea salt and freshly ground black pepper

3 Tbsp (45 mL) canola oil

6–8 anchovies

1 large burrata cheese ball (keep whole)

Zest from 1 lemon

6–8 basil leaves

I told you about my love for Italy and shared with you some of my experiences there. This recipe's inspiration comes from my visits to seaside towns like Positano, where fresh daily seafood is paired with ripe produce, making for a killer combination.

1. Prepare an ice bath in a bucket or the sink. 2. To cook the lobster, in a large saucepan over high heat, bring 12 cups (3 L) of cold, salted water to a boil. Using tongs, submerge the lobster, head first, in the boiling water, and cook, covered, for 8 to 10 minutes, or until the lobster turns bright red. Using tongs again, remove the lobster from the water and place it in the ice bath for 5 to 10 minutes to stop the cooking process. Then, using a large chef's knife or kitchen shears, carefully crack and break down the shell and remove as much meat as possible. Roughly chop the meat. 3. In a large mixing bowl, mix the lobster meat with the spinach, tomatoes, olive oil, agave nectar, and salt and pepper to taste. Mix well to combine. Refrigerate, covered, until ready to serve. 4. Line a plate with paper towels. 5. In a small saucepan, heat the canola oil over high heat. Using a metal slotted spoon, carefully lower the anchovies into the hot oil and fry for 20 to 30 seconds, or until they're crispy but not burnt. Using the slotted spoon, remove the fried anchovies from the hot oil and place them on the prepared plate to absorb any excess oil. 6. Place the lobster meat mixture in the center of a large serving platter. In the middle of the meat, place the burrata cheese ball and garnish it with the crispy anchovies, lemon zest, and fresh basil leaves. 7. Cut open the burrata and let the cheese ooze over the lobster and anchovies! This recipe is best enjoyed right away.

Dinner

LOBSTER MAC-DADDY BURGER

SERVES 2

1 live lobster (1 ½ lb/680 g)

½ lb (225 g) medium ground beef

Kosher salt and freshly ground black pepper

1 Tbsp (15 mL) canola oil

1 small white onion, finely diced

4 sesame seed burger buns

¼ cup (60 mL) Thousand Island dressing

1 Tbsp (15 mL) green relish

½ cup (125 mL) finely chopped iceberg lettuce

2 thin slices aged cheddar cheese

1 kosher pickle, cut into thin slices

This surf and turf burger absolutely rocks! It makes me think of the special treats I'd crave as a kid, and this was definitely one of my top choices. I love how food can quickly transport you to another time and place simply because of a delicious memory.

1. Prepare an ice bath in a bucket or the sink. 2. To cook the lobster, in a large saucepan over high heat, bring 12 cups (3 L) of cold, salted water to a boil. Using tongs, submerge the lobster, head first, in the boiling water, and cook, covered, for 8 to 10 minutes, or until the lobster turns bright red. Using tongs again, remove the lobster from the water and place it in the ice bath for 5 to 10 minutes to stop the cooking process. Then, using a large chef's knife or kitchen shears, carefully crack and break down the shell and remove as much meat shell as possible. Roughly chop the meat and then set it aside. 3. In a medium-size mixing bowl, combine the ground beef with salt and pepper to taste. Using your hands, form four equal-sized hamburger patties, about ¼-inch (6 mm) thick, and set aside at room temperature. 4. In a large, nonstick skillet, heat the canola oil over medium-high heat. Add the onions and sauté for 2 to 3 minutes, or until soft and translucent. Place each burger patty in the skillet with the onions and cook for 1 to 2 minutes per side, or until cooked through. Transfer the burgers and onions to a plate and set aside at room temperature. 5. Clean the skillet and heat it again over medium-high heat. Toast each bun, bottom and top, for 15 to 30 seconds, or until slightly browned. 6. In a small mixing bowl, mix together the Thousand Island dressing and relish. 7. On a clean work surface, lay out two burger bun bottoms and spoon the dressing sauce overtop each one. Top with a small spoonful of cooked onions, some lettuce, a cheese slice, and two or three slices of pickle. Place one burger patty and one-quarter of the lobster meat on top. Place a second bottom bun on top of the lobster meat and repeat the previous steps, but close the burger with the top portion of the bun. Do it all again for the second burger. You'll end up with two burger tops that you aren't using, which you can save for later or discard. 8. Serve with some crispy french fries if you're looking for a side dish!

Quick & Easy

SERVES 2–4

1 live lobster (1 ½ lb/680 g)

Juice from 1 lime

1 Tbsp (15 mL) soy sauce

1 tsp (5 mL) fish sauce

1 package wonton wrappers

2 cups (500 mL) canola oil

Kosher salt

2 large ripe avocados

1 large Roma tomato, diced

1 yellow bell pepper, diced

1 red bell pepper, diced

1 Tbsp (15 mL) sweet paprika

4 Tbsp (60 mL) Sriracha Mayo
(page 226)

4 green onions, finely chopped

¼ cup (60 mL) white and
black sesame seeds

LOBSTER POKE WONTON NACHOS

Poke originates in Hawaii. It's raw fish or shellfish cut into pieces and served over salad, noodles, or rice. It's incredibly delicious—and good for you too. I visited a small poke food stall when I was in New York recently. I think we waited in line for close to an hour. Crazy, right? Maybe, but it was everything I dreamed it would be and more, and therefore worth the wait. Get on the poke train, my friends. I love mine with my spicy, creamy Sriracha Mayo and homemade wonton chips.

1. Prepare an ice bath in a bucket or the sink. 2. To cook the lobster, in a large saucepan over high heat, bring 12 cups (3 L) of cold, salted water to a boil. Using tongs, submerge the lobster, head first, in the boiling water, and cook, covered, for 8 to 10 minutes, or until the lobster turns bright red. Using tongs again, remove the lobster from the water and place it in the ice bath for 5 to 10 minutes to stop the cooking process. Then, using a large chef's knife or kitchen shears, carefully crack and break down the shell and remove as much meat as possible. Roughly chop the meat and place it in a large mixing bowl. 3. Add the lime juice, soy sauce, and fish sauce to the lobster meat and mix to combine. Cover and refrigerate for 1 hour to chill thoroughly. 4. In the meantime, prepare and fry the wontons. In a large saucepan or deep-fryer, bring the canola oil to 350–375°F (180–190°C) over medium-high heat. Use a cooking thermometer to check the temperature. Line a baking tray with paper towels. 5. Working in small batches, use tongs to carefully lower the wonton wrappers into the hot oil, and fry for 45 seconds to 1 minute, or until crispy and evenly golden brown, flipping midway through. Using a slotted spoon, remove the fried wontons from the hot oil and place them on the baking tray to absorb any excess oil. Season with a pinch of kosher salt and then set aside. Watch these carefully as they fry extremely quickly—you do not want them to burn! 6. Pit the avocados and then cut them into ¼-inch (6 mm) cubes. Place them in a medium-size bowl and add the tomatoes and both bell peppers. Mix well. 7. On a large serving platter, stack the fried wontons and season with paprika. Top with the chilled lobster meat mixture and tomato mixture. Garnish with Sriracha Mayo, green onions, and sesame seeds.

Lunch

SERVES 2

1 live lobster (1 ½–2 lb/680–900 g)

1 celery stalk, finely chopped

Juice of ½ lemon

1 Tbsp (15 mL) full-fat mayonnaise

1 tsp (5 mL) Old Bay Seasoning or Seafood Seasoning

1 cup (250 mL) canola oil

1 large Spanish or yellow onion

1 cup (250 mL) all-purpose flour

1 tsp (5 mL) baking soda

2 top-sliced hot dog buns, buttered both sides

¼ cup (60 mL) finely chopped chives

Potato chips, for serving

Pickles, for serving

MATTY'S JACKED-UP LOBSTER ROLL

This recipe is the one I'm most thankful for. It's been the perfect dish for a pop-up shop, an inspiration for my restaurants, something delicious for the media to sink their teeth into, and a point of reference for new business development ideas. I absolutely cherish these rolls. Many people have made lobster rolls but I truly believe my success comes down to two things—my use of high-quality, fresh ingredients and my passion for seafood.

1. Prepare an ice bath in a bucket or the sink. 2. To cook the lobster, in a large stockpot over high heat, bring 12 cups (3 L) of salted, cold water to a boil. Using tongs, submerge the lobster, head first, in the boiling water, and cook for 7 to 8 minutes per pound (450 g). Using the tongs again, remove the lobster from the stockpot, and plunge into the ice bath for 5 to 10 minutes to stop the cooking process. 3. Using a lobster cracker or the side of a large knife, smack the lobster shell until it cracks in several places. Remove the meat from the claws, tail, and knuckle. Cut the tail with a knife or scissors to access the meat. Coarsely chop all the lobster meat and place it in a mixing bowl. Add the celery, lemon juice, mayonnaise, and seafood seasoning. Mix well to combine and then set aside in the fridge. 4. In a small saucepan or deep-fryer, bring the canola oil to 350–375°F (180–190°C) over medium-high heat. Use a cooking thermometer to check the temperature. 5. Meanwhile, finely slice the onion. 6. In a small, shallow bowl, combine the flour and baking soda for dredging. Line a plate with paper towels. 7. Dredge the finely sliced onions in the bowl of flour and then shake off any excess. Using tongs and working in batches, carefully place the coated onion pieces in the hot oil and fry for 15 to 20 seconds, until crispy and brown. Using a slotted spoon, remove the crispy fried onions and place them on the prepared plate to absorb any excess oil. Set aside. 8. On a hot grill top or in a skillet, toast each side of the buttered buns. Spoon the lobster mixture into the buns. Garnish with crispy fried onions and chives. Serve the lobster rolls with chips and pickles on the side.

Dinner

MATTY'S LOBSTER NEWBURG

SERVES 4

2 lemons

1 orange

1 bay leaf

Kosher salt

4 live lobsters (1¼–
1½ lb/565–680 g each)

½ cup (125 mL) unsalted
butter

¼ cup (60 mL) finely chopped
shallots

1½ cups (375 mL) light (18%)
cream or half-and-half

3 Tbsp (45 mL) dark rum

Pinch of sweet paprika

1 tsp (5 mL) cayenne pepper

1 tsp (5 mL) ground nutmeg

3 large egg yolks

¼ cup (60 mL) chopped curly
parsley, for garnish

I must say that this recipe, from the late 1800s, takes the cake! Its rich, bold flavors seem to keep going and going when you eat it. If you're looking for a classic lobster dish for a great romantic dinner, this is it. Funnily enough, I've never made this for a romantic dinner for Dana, but I have made it for many people at my restaurants. Presentation is everything, so be sure to use the body of the lobster as the serving vessel. And get your cell phone out, because this dish makes for eye-catching Instagram pictures.

1. Slice the lemons and the orange in half widthwise. **2.** Next, make a court bouillon. Fill a very large stockpot with 8 ½ quarts (8 L) of cold water, add the lemons, oranges, bay leaf, and a healthy-sized pinch of kosher salt. Cover the stockpot with a lid and bring the liquid to a boil over high heat. Once boiling, use tongs to add the live lobsters (all if you can or working in batches if you must). Cook for 7 to 8 minutes; the lobsters will be bright red. **3.** Using tongs again, carefully remove each of the lobsters from the stockpot and place them on a cutting board to cool slightly. Discard the cooking liquid. Once cooled, cut the tail sections in half lengthwise, keeping the tails connected to the bodies. You'll eventually use the empty tail/shell portion like a plate. Gently remove the tail meat only. Roughly chop it and set it aside in a bowl at room temperature. Carefully crack each of the claws, keeping the meat intact and inside the claws. Set the claws and lobster bodies aside at room temperature. **4.** In a large saucepan, melt the butter over medium heat. Then add the shallots and cook for approximately 1 minute. Add the cream, rum, and paprika, stirring constantly until they've fully integrated. Add the cayenne pepper and nutmeg, stirring to combine. **5.** Place the egg yolks in a small bowl. Add 1 Tbsp (15 mL) of the hot cream liquid and stir it into the egg yolks to temper them. Add another 1 Tbsp (15 mL) of the hot cream and continue to stir. Be careful—if your liquid is too hot or you add it too quickly, it'll scramble the eggs. **6.** Once the egg yolks have warmed up, slowly stir the mixture back into the saucepan with the cream. Continue to stir, gradually adding the chopped lobster meat. Cook for approximately 2 minutes to warm the meat through. **7.** Place each lobster body on a large plate with the cracked claws and split tail. Gently spoon the cream sauce into the empty tail area of the lobster. Garnish with the chopped parsley and serve immediately.

Dinner

SERVES 2–4

2 live lobsters (1 ½ lb/680 g each)

½ cup (125 mL) cornstarch

6 green onions

¼ cup (60 mL) canola oil

4 cloves garlic, finely diced

1 Tbsp (15 mL) minced peeled fresh ginger

1 tsp (5 mL) Chinese five-spice

1 cup (250 mL) vegetable stock

¼ cup (60 mL) soy sauce

¼ cup (60 mL) rice wine

1 Tbsp (15 mL) fish sauce

1 tsp (5 mL) granulated sugar

1 package (17 ½ oz/500 g) lo-mein noodles, cooked as per package's instructions

1 cup (250 mL) fresh bean sprouts

SPADINA SPECIAL CANTONESE LOBSTER LO-MEIN

Spadina Avenue is the site not only of Toronto's Chinatown, but also of countless late-night meals I've had over the years. On any random night, you'll see some of Toronto's best cooks and chefs dining in the small, packed restaurants that line the street. I love getting to know the staff at these restaurants, including my favorite, Rol San, and asking them questions about their cuisine. Some of the best advice I've received over the years is to let the flavors bind together. Fresh garlic, ginger, and green onions, plus any other Asian spices you may like to add, create a great base for almost any sauce.

1. Prepare an ice bath in a bucket or the sink. 2. To cook the lobsters, in a very large saucepan over high heat, bring 6 quarts (6 L) of salted, cold water to a boil. Using tongs, submerge the lobsters, head first, in the boiling water, and cook, covered, for approximately 8 to 10 minutes, or until they turn bright red. Using tongs again, remove the lobsters from the water and place them in the ice bath for 5 to 10 minutes to stop the cooking process. Then, using a large chef's knife or kitchen shears, carefully crack and break down the shells and remove as much meat as possible. Roughly chop the meat and place it in a large bowl. Add the cornstarch and mix to coat the lobster pieces. 3. Finely chop four of the green onions and place them in a small bowl. Chop the remaining two green onions and place them in a separate small bowl. 4. In a large, deep saucepan or wok, heat the canola oil over medium-high heat. Add the four finely chopped green onions, garlic, ginger, and Chinese five-spice. Cook, stirring constantly, for 1 to 2 minutes, until fragrant. 5. Add the coated lobster pieces to the saucepan and stir to mix all the ingredients together. Turn down the heat to medium-low, cover, and cook for 3 to 4 minutes, stirring once or twice. 6. In a medium-size mixing bowl, combine the vegetable stock, soy sauce, rice wine, fish sauce, and sugar. Mix well. Add the sauce to the saucepan, mix to combine, and cook for 1 to 2 minutes, or until heated through. Add the remaining two green onions and the bean sprouts. Stir well. 7. Place the cooked lo-mein noodles on a large serving platter and top with the hot lobster mixture. Serve immediately.

SERVES 4

1 live lobster (1 ½ lb/680 g)

18 oz (500 g) lean ground beef

¼ cup (60 mL) Italian breadcrumbs

1 large egg

2 Tbsp (30 mL) tomato paste

1 Tbsp (15 mL) hot sauce

1 small bunch of fresh mint, finely chopped, divided

1 tsp (5 mL) ground cumin

Kosher salt and freshly ground black pepper

2 Tbsp (30 mL) canola oil

4 (8-inch/20 cm) flour tortillas

4 Tbsp (60 mL) Sriracha Mayo (page 226)

NOTE: If you want to ditch the carb-loaded flour tortilla wrap, reach for the low-calorie lettuce wraps instead.

SRIRACHA SURF & TURF TACOS

My inspiration for this dish comes from walking the small, winding streets of Europe. It seems every city has its own take on hand-held walking foods, and I always enjoy these snacks when I travel. I figured, let's combine two of my favorite foods, beef and lobster, and put them into one delicious edible snack!

1. Preheat the oven to 400°F (200°C). Prepare an ice bath in a bucket or the sink. 2. To cook the lobster, in a large saucepan over high heat, bring 12 cups (3 L) of salted, cold water to a boil. Using tongs, submerge the lobster, head first, in the boiling water, and cook, covered, for 8 to 10 minutes, or until it turns bright red. Using tongs again, remove the lobster from the water and place it in the ice bath for 5 to 10 minutes to stop the cooking process. Then, using a large chef's knife or kitchen shears, carefully crack and break down the shell and remove as much meat as possible. Roughly chop the meat and set it aside. 3. In a large mixing bowl, place the ground beef, breadcrumbs, egg, tomato paste, hot sauce, three-quarters of the mint, cumin, and salt and pepper to taste. Using your hands, mix everything together well and then roll out 12 to 16 evenly sized meatballs, about 1 inch (2.5 cm) in diameter. 4. In a large skillet, heat the canola oil over medium-high heat. Sauté each meatball for approximately 1 to 2 minutes, turning them often so they brown evenly. Transfer the meatballs to a baking tray and bake for 5 to 7 minutes, or until cooked through. 5. Turn down the oven to 350°F (180°C). Wrap the tortillas in aluminum foil and then put them in the hot oven for 1 to 2 minutes to warm them and make them pliable. 6. Lay the warm tortillas out on a flat surface. Spoon 1 to 2 Tbsp (15 to 30 mL) of Sriracha Mayo in the middle of each one, followed by three to four meatballs and one-quarter of the warm lobster meat. Garnish with the extra chopped mint and serve immediately.

MUSSELS

Brunch

SERVES 4

1 lb (450 g) live mussels

1 medium white onion, diced

2 Tbsp (30 mL) canola oil

4 cloves garlic, minced

½ cup (125 mL) chopped
flat-leaf parsley, plus more for
garnish

2 bay leaves

1 tsp (5 mL) brown sugar

1 tsp (5 mL) ground cumin

1 tsp (5 mL) fresh oregano
leaves

1 cup (250 mL) dry white wine

1 tsp (5 mL) Worcestershire
sauce

2 cups (500 mL) diced
tomatoes

½ lb (225 g) fresh or frozen
(thawed) sea scallops

4 snow crab or king crab legs,
cooked, for garnish

Kosher salt

CHOPPINO

Choppino originated in San Francisco, where its ingredients changed often because it was made with whatever the fishermen caught that day. The one constant of a great choppino, though, is a wine and tomato broth base. I wanted to include my rustic take on it here, as it's simple, full of flavor, and great for sharing.

1. Clean the mussels under cold, running water. Remove any hair connected to the mussels and discard any mussels that are completely or even slightly open. Set aside in the fridge. 2. In a large saucepan over medium-high heat, cook the onions in the canola oil for 2 to 3 minutes, or until they're soft and translucent. Add the garlic, parsley, bay leaves, sugar, cumin, and oregano. Cook, stirring constantly, for 4 to 6 minutes, or until you can smell the beautiful aromatics of the herbs and spices. 3. Add 4 cups (1 L) of cold water, the white wine, and Worcestershire sauce. Cook for 10 to 12 minutes, stirring occasionally, and allowing the mixture to reduce slightly. Turn down the heat to medium and then add the tomatoes. Cook, covered, for an additional 10 minutes. 4. Place the mussels and scallops in the saucepan, cover, and cook for another 3 to 6 minutes, or until the mussels have opened. Discard any mussels that do not open. Using kitchen shears, carefully cut through the crab shell to expose the meat, and cut the legs into 3-inch (8 cm) pieces. Add the pieces of crab legs to the saucepan and mix well to combine with the other ingredients. Check seasoning and add salt to taste. Warm the leg pieces all the way through for about 1 minute. 5. Divide the choppino between four serving bowls and garnish with a little fresh parsley. This is amazing with crusty bread!

Quick & Easy

SERVES 2–4

2 lb (900 g) live mussels

2 Tbsp (30 mL) canola oil

1 medium white onion, finely diced

4 cloves garlic, finely minced

1 cup (250 mL) canned cannellini beans, drained and rinsed

1 lb (450 g) spicy chorizo sausages

2 Roma tomatoes, coarsely chopped

½ cup (125 mL) dry white wine

Pinch of ground cumin

½ cup (125 mL) flat-leaf parsley, coarsely chopped

Pinch of sweet paprika

MUSSELS & CHORIZO

Mussels are great shellfish to eat. Not only are they one of the most sustainable seafoods on the planet, they're also quite affordable, which makes them perfect for feeding a lot of people. The next time you have a large friend or family gathering, try this mussel recipe. I'm sure it will be a huge hit.

1. Clean the mussels under cold, running water. Remove any hair connected to the mussels and discard any mussels that are completely or even slightly open. Set aside in the fridge. 2. In a large, deep skillet or saucepan, heat the canola oil over medium-high heat. Sauté the onions for 2 to 3 minutes, or until soft and translucent. Add the garlic and then the cannellini beans, and stir to combine. 3. Meanwhile, cut open the sausage casing and remove the chorizo. Add it to the saucepan and then use a wooden spoon to break it down. Cook the mixture, stirring occasionally, for an additional 2 to 3 minutes. 4. Add ¼ cup (60 mL) of cold water, the tomatoes, wine, and cumin. Cook, stirring, for 2 to 3 minutes to allow the flavors to combine. 5. Add the mussels, cover, and cook for 3 to 5 minutes, or until the mussels have opened. Discard any mussels that do not open. 6. Spoon into serving bowls and garnish with the parsley and paprika.

Dinner

SERVES 2

2 lb (900 g) live mussels

2 Tbsp (30 mL) extra-virgin olive oil

1 medium white onion, finely chopped

2 cloves garlic, crushed

1 cup (250 mL) coarsely chopped Roma tomatoes

½ cup (125 mL) dry white wine

Kosher salt and freshly ground black pepper

¼ 16-oz/455 g package of spaghetti noodles

2 Tbsp (30 mL) squid ink (see note)

¼ cup (60 mL) finely chopped flat-leaf parsley

NOTE: Buy the squid ink from quality fish markets or specialty grocery stores. If you can't find squid ink, try cuttlefish ink instead. It's less expensive but gives off more of a brownish than blue-black color.

CURRIED MUSSELS & SQUID INK SPAGHETTI

I'm always working on my plating and presentation skills. This is one dish that I've played around with a lot to get it just right. The different pops in color make it a real stunner. Have fun making and plating this spaghetti. I'd love to see what you come up with! Tag me in your pictures (@mattdeanpettit) and use the hashtag #TheGreatShellfishCookbook.

1. Clean the mussels under cold, running water. Remove any hair connected to the mussels and discard any mussels that are completely or even slightly open. 2. To cook the mussels, place a large saucepan with 2 cups (500 mL) of cold water over high heat. Cover the saucepan and bring to a boil. Add the mussels, cover with a lid again, and steam for 2 to 3 minutes, or until most of the mussels have opened. Drain the mussels and discard any unopened shells. Let the mussels cool enough to handle comfortably. 3. Once the mussels have cooled, grip the top shell in one hand and the bottom shell in the other hand, and give a small pull to detach the shells. Using your fingers or a small fork, remove the meat from the shell and place it in a small bowl. Repeat with the remaining mussels. You should have about 2 cups (500 mL) of meat. 4. In a nonstick skillet, heat the olive oil over medium-high heat. Sauté the onions for 2 to 3 minutes, or until soft and translucent. Add the garlic and then the tomatoes and wine, and cook, uncovered and stirring occasionally, for 8 to 10 minutes, or until the mixture has reduced by about two-thirds. Add salt and pepper to taste. 5. While the mixture reduces, cook the spaghetti in salted boiling water until al dente. 6. Place a few drops of the squid ink in a small bowl and use a pastry brush to make a nice long, wide ink stripe on each serving plate. 7. Drain the pasta and return it to the pot. Add the remaining squid ink to the cooked pasta and mix thoroughly. Add the mussel meat and the sauce, stir to combine, and heat everything on medium-high for approximately 1 minute to bring to temperature. 8. Carefully place the spaghetti and mussels in the middle of each plate so that the brushed ink is showing on both sides of the dish. Top with a sprinkling of parsley. Remember, we eat with our eyes first!

Quick & Easy

SERVES 2–4

3 lb (1.3 kg) live mussels

4 tsp (20 mL) sesame oil

2 cloves garlic, finely chopped

1 Tbsp (15 mL) dried chilies

2 tsp (10 mL) finely chopped
fresh ginger

¼ cup (60 mL) soy sauce

¼ cup (60 mL) lime juice
(about 2 limes)

¼ cup (60 mL) chicken broth

1 cup (250 mL) cornstarch

1 Tbsp (15 mL) baking powder

2 large eggs

2 cups (500 mL) canola oil

¼ cup (60 mL) toasted sesame
seeds

¼ cup (60 mL) finely chopped
green onions

GENERAL TSO MUSSELS

One of my favorite places in Toronto is Chinatown, located along Spadina Avenue. I enjoy just getting lost, walking, tasting, smelling, and seeing so many great fruits, vegetables, and some items that remain unfamiliar to me even now! There's nothing better than going on a culinary food tour whenever you can, even if it's at home. This dish is one I always seek out while on these types of walks: the magical combination of sweet, spicy, and savory is perfect.

1. Clean the mussels under cold, running water. Remove any hair connected to the mussels and discard any mussels that are completely or even slightly open. 2. Fill a large saucepan with 10 cups (2.5 L) of cold water and bring it to a boil over high heat. Cook the mussels for approximately 1 minute, just to open the shells for now—you'll continue to cook the meat later. Remove the mussels from the saucepan. Once the mussels have cooled, grip the top shell in one hand and the bottom shell in the other hand, and give a small pull to detach the shells. Using your fingers or a small fork, remove the meat from the shell and place it in a small bowl. Repeat with the remaining mussels. 3. In a medium-size sauté pan over high heat, place the sesame oil, followed by the garlic, chilies, and ginger, and then the soy sauce, lime juice, and chicken broth. Whisk the ingredients together and then turn down the heat to low. Simmer, uncovered, for 4 to 5 minutes, stirring occasionally, or until the sauce has reduced by half. Once reduced, remove from the heat and set aside. 4. In a medium-size mixing bowl, combine the cornstarch and baking powder. Slowly whisk in the eggs to create a batter. Set aside at room temperature. 5. In a medium-size saucepan over medium-high heat, bring the canola oil to 350°F (180°C). Use a cooking thermometer to check the temperature. Line a plate with paper towels. 6. Working in small batches, coat the mussel meats in batter, letting any excess drip off, and then use tongs to lower them into the hot oil. Fry the mussel meats for 2 to 3 minutes, or until crispy and golden brown. Using a metal slotted spoon, remove them from the oil and place them on the prepared plate to absorb any excess oil. Let the oil come back up to temperature before proceeding with the next batch. 7. Place the fried mussels on a platter, or divide them among individual serving bowls, and pour the sauce overtop, ensuring that all the mussels are evenly coated. Garnish with the toasted sesame seeds and green onions.

Dinner

SERVES 2–4

1 cup (250 mL) Spanish or Arborio rice

1 lb (450 g) live mussels

½ lb (225 g) shrimp, spot prawns, or tiger shrimp, raw with shells on (see note)

2 Tbsp (30 mL) extra-virgin olive oil

1 large red onion, finely diced

4 cloves garlic, minced

1 cup (250 mL) green beans, cut into 1-inch (2.5 cm) pieces then measured

1 cup (250 mL) chopped Roma tomatoes

1 Tbsp (15 mL) capers

1 Tbsp (15 mL) dried saffron

1 Tbsp (15 mL) ground cinnamon

1 tsp (5 mL) chili flakes

½ cup (125 mL) dry white wine

¾ cup (175 mL) vegetable or chicken stock

½ cup (125 mL) warm water

2 raw or frozen and thawed lobster tails, cut into 1-inch (2.5 cm) pieces

1 Tbsp (15 mL) sweet paprika, for garnish

MATTY'S SPANISH VACAY PAELLA

I fell in love with paella when I first traveled to Spain. Paella originates from the beautiful city of Valencia, on the southeastern coast. Almost every restaurant there has their own individual family recipe for paella. You'll find seafood, chicken, duck, rabbit, snail, and vegetable paella. The key to cooking a great paella (which is kind of like risotto) is to not overcook the rice. Keep an eye on it as you cook, and be sure to stir. And enjoy! Or, as the Spanish say, *buen provecho!*

1. Place the Spanish rice in a bowl of cold water to soak for approximately 10 minutes. 2. Clean the mussels under cold, running water. Remove any hair connected to the mussels and discard any mussels that are completely or even slightly open. Set aside. 3. Run your choice of shrimp, prawns, or tiger shrimp under cold, running water to clean them. Set aside in the fridge. You'll be cooking these with the shells on, as that's where the flavor is. 4. In a large skillet, heat the olive oil over medium-high heat. Add the onions and garlic and cook for 3 to 5 minutes, or until soft and translucent. Add the green beans and tomatoes and stir well to combine. Add the capers, saffron, cinnamon, and chili flakes. Stir again to combine and coat the vegetables. Let them cook for 2 to 3 minutes. 5. Meanwhile, drain the rice. Add the rice and wine to the vegetables and bring to a boil. Add the stock and water as well. Using a wooden spoon, stir constantly as it returns to a boil to ensure that the rice is fully covered in sauce. Once the mixture is boiling, turn down the heat to medium-low and simmer, uncovered and stirring frequently, for 25 to 35 minutes, or until the rice is al dente. 6. Add the shrimp, mussels, and lobster to the skillet, cover, and cook for 5 to 7 minutes, or until the seafood is cooked and opaque, and most of the mussels are open. Discard any mussels that do not open. 7. Sprinkle the mixture with sweet paprika while it's still in the skillet. Serve immediately in bowls.

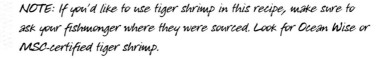

NOTE: If you'd like to use tiger shrimp in this recipe, make sure to ask your fishmonger where they were sourced. Look for Ocean Wise or MSC-certified tiger shrimp.

Party!

SERVES 4–6

2 lb (900 g) live mussels

4 large eggs

3 cups (750 mL)
  Italian breadcrumbs

1 cup (250 mL) canola oil

½ cup (125 mL) flat-leaf
  parsley, for garnish

2 medium lemons, quartered

Matty's Seafood Cocktail
  Sauce, for dipping (page
  225)

Tartar sauce, for dipping

GAME DAY FRIED MUSSELS

Blue 24, Blue 24, hut hut hut! I am a huge sports fan, and football is certainly one of my favorites. There's nothing better than watching the Big Game and eating these treats. So, skip the nachos next weekend and try these instead. I promise you won't be disappointed. This recipe doubles easily for a big gathering. Let's go, Buffalo!

1. Clean the mussels under cold, running water. Remove any hair connected to the mussels and discard any mussels that are completely or even slightly open. 2. Fill a large stockpot with 8 ½ quarts (8 L) of cold water and bring it to a boil over high heat. Cook the mussels for approximately 1 minute, just to open the shells for now—you'll continue to cook the meat later. Discard any mussels that don't open. Once the mussels have cooled, grip the top shell in one hand and the bottom shell in the other hand, and give a small pull to detach the shells. Using your fingers or a small fork, remove the meat from the shell and place it in a small bowl. Repeat with the remaining mussels. 3. Prepare a dredging station by beating the eggs in a shallow, medium-size bowl and placing the breadcrumbs in a separate shallow bowl. Dredge all the mussel meat pieces in the beaten egg and then in the breadcrumbs. Shake off any excess breadcrumbs, place the mussel meats on a baking tray, and set aside at room temperature. 4. In a medium-size saucepan, over medium-high heat, heat the canola oil to 375°F (190°C), checking with a cooking thermometer. Line a plate with paper towels. 5. Fry the mussel meat pieces for 2 to 3 minutes, or until golden brown. You may have to do this in batches, and allow the oil to come back up to temperature in between batches. Transfer the fried mussels to the prepared plate to absorb any excess oil. 6. Place the fried mussels on a large serving platter and garnish with the parsley and lemon quarters. Dunk the fried mussels into Matty's Seafood Cocktail Sauce or tartar sauce. Yum!

Brunch

SERVES 2–4

1½ lb (680 g) live mussels

1 cup (250 mL) shredded Spanish Manchego cheese

½ cup (125 mL) full-fat sour cream

¼ cup (60 mL) heavy (35%) cream

1 tsp (5 mL) chili flakes

1 bunch chives, finely diced

MELTED CHEESY MUSSELS

I think I may love cheese as much as I love lobster (as you may have realized from some of the other recipes in this book). In this recipe, I like to use Spanish Manchego, which is made from sheep's milk. It's a medium-hard cheese and packed with flavor. Typically, it's aged for a minimum of 60 days and up to 2 years. If you love cheese as much as I do, and if you find yourself visiting Toronto, be sure to seek out my good friend and maître fromager Afrim Pristine, the co-owner of Cheese Boutique. His place is a real treasure—it's filled with every kind of cheese imaginable, as well as cured meats, crackers, hot foods, and more! He even contributed a recipe to this cookbook (see page 137).

1. Preheat the oven to the high broiler setting and place one of the oven racks in the second-highest position. Line a large baking tray with parchment paper.
2. Clean the mussels under cold, running water. Remove any hair connected to the mussels and discard any mussels that are completely or even slightly open. Set aside. 3. Fill a large saucepan with 1 cup (250 mL) of cold water, cover with a lid, and bring to a boil over high heat. Add the mussels, cover, and steam for 2 to 3 minutes, or until all the mussels have opened. Discard any mussels that do not open. 4. Once the mussels have cooled, grip the top shell in one hand and the bottom shell in the other hand, and give a small pull to detach only the top shell. Repeat with the remaining mussels. Discard the top shell of each mussel, leaving just the meat in the bottom half of the shell. Place the mussels on the prepared baking tray. 5. In a large mixing bowl, combine the cheese, sour cream, heavy cream, and chili flakes. 6. Spoon 1 tsp (5 mL) of the cheese mixture into each half mussel, using the back of a separate spoon to pack it in tightly. 7. Place the mussels under the broiler for 3 to 5 minutes, or until the cheese is bubbly and golden brown. Watch closely so the cheese doesn't burn. 8. Remove the mussels from the broiler, transfer them to a serving platter, and garnish with diced chives. Serve these hot.

Brunch

SERVES 2

2 lb (900 g) mussels

2 large Yukon Gold or russet potatoes, peeled and cut into matchsticks

3 cups + 1 Tbsp (765 mL) canola oil, divided

Kosher salt and freshly cracked black pepper

2 cloves garlic, minced

1 shallot, minced

1 lemon

½ cup (125 mL) of your favorite lager

1 Tbsp (15 mL) unsalted butter

1 Tbsp (15 mL) fresh thyme leaves

2 Tbsp (30 mL) chopped flat-leaf parsley

1 small baguette, warmed

MOULES FRITES

If you've ever been to a café in Bruges or a bistro in Paris, you'll know that this dish, or versions similar to it, are classic staples. I enjoy working with classic dishes and putting my own spin on them, but in this case, the tried and true classic wins every time.

1. Clean the mussels under cold, running water. Remove any hair connected to the mussels and discard any mussels that are completely or even slightly open. Set aside in the fridge until needed. **2.** In a deep sauté pan or medium-size saucepan, heat 3 cups (750 mL) of canola oil to 375°–400°F (180°–200°C). Use a cooking thermometer to check the temperature. Line a plate with paper towels. **3.** Once the oil is at temperature, use a metal slotted spoon to add the matchstick potatoes in small batches to avoid overcrowding the pan. Let the potatoes fry for 5 minutes. Using the slotted spoon, carefully remove the fries from the oil and place them on the prepared plate to absorb any excess oil. Let the oil come back up to temperature in between batches. **4.** Once the fries have cooled, work in small batches again and repeat the frying process for 3 to 5 minutes to get a crisp golden-brown outside with a soft texture in the middle. Remove the fries and place them on a plate lined with fresh paper towels. Sprinkle with salt to taste. Keep the fries loosely covered with aluminum foil, or put them in a 200°F (95°C) oven (or as low as your oven can go) to stay warm. **5.** In a large saucepan, heat the remaining 1 Tbsp (15 mL) of canola oil over medium-high heat. Add the garlic, shallots, and a squeeze of lemon juice, and cook for 2 to 3 minutes, or until soft. Add the mussels, beer, butter, and then the thyme. Cover with a lid and cook, stirring once or twice, for 2 to 3 minutes, or until all the mussels have opened. Discard any mussels that do not open. **6.** Ladle the mussel broth and mussels into serving bowls. Garnish with the parsley and pepper to taste. Serve with the warm baguette and the frites!

SMOKED MUSSEL ARANCINI

SERVES 4–6

4 cups (1 L) chicken broth

1 Tbsp (15 mL) olive oil

2 cloves garlic, minced

1½ cups (375 mL) Arborio rice

2 cans (6 oz/170 g each) smoked mussels, drained and patted dry

½ cup (125 mL) grated Parmigiano-Reggiano cheese

2 cups (500 mL) Italian breadcrumbs

1 cup (250 mL) all-purpose flour

4 large eggs, whisked

¼ cup (60 mL) full-fat mayonnaise

Juice of 1 lemon

Sea salt

4 cups (1 L) canola oil

A COUPLE OF QUICK TIPS FOR MAKING THE RISOTTO: Don't wash the rice before you cook it. You want the starch to remain on the surface, so that the dish will become creamy. The risotto should not be gummy or dense, so the rice should only be cooked al dente. This recipe doubles easily for larger gatherings too.

I like to use smoked mussels in this as they're much more flavorful when they're canned. Smoked mussels can vary in quality, so look for ones sold at specialty grocery stores.

1. In a medium-size saucepan over medium-high heat, bring the broth to a boil, uncovered. Cover, turn down the heat to low, and simmer. **2.** In a medium-size skillet, heat the olive oil over medium heat. Add the garlic and cook, stirring occasionally, for 2 to 3 minutes. Add the rice and cook, stirring, for another 2 to 3 minutes, until it releases a nutty aroma and looks slightly toasted. **3.** Add ½ cup (125 mL) of the broth to the rice, stirring constantly with a wooden spoon until the liquid is absorbed. Continue to add the broth, ½ cup (125 mL) at a time, stirring constantly and allowing the liquid to absorb before adding the next. Cook the mixture for 16 to 18 minutes, or until the rice is al dente and creamy. **4.** Add the Parmigiano-Reggiano cheese and stir to combine. Turn off the heat and allow the mixture to cool completely for 1 to 2 hours, or until you can handle it comfortably. **5.** Dampen your hands and use them to roll 2 Tbsp (30 mL) of the rice mixture into a ball—this will be your arancini. Press your thumb into the center of the ball, making a small indentation. Insert a smoked mussel in the hole and then roll the rice mixture back into a ball to enclose it. Set the rice ball aside on a baking tray lined with parchment paper, and repeat the process with the remaining mixture. You should have about 12 to 14 arancini when you're done. **6.** Cover the arancini loosely with plastic wrap and refrigerate for 30 minutes. **7.** Set up a dredging station with one bowl of breadcrumbs, one bowl of flour, and one bowl of whisked eggs. Roll each rice ball in the flour, dip in the egg wash, and then in the breadcrumbs. Place the balls back on the baking tray and refrigerate, covered, for 30 minutes. **8.** In a small bowl, mix together the mayonnaise, lemon juice, and salt. Set aside. **9.** Line a plate with paper towels. **10.** In a large, deep skillet or saucepan, add enough canola oil to come 2 inches (5 cm) up the sides of the pan, to shallow-fry the arancini. Heat it over medium-high, until it reaches about 350°F (180°C). Working in small batches, and allowing the oil to come back up to temperature in between batches, use a metal slotted spoon to place the rice balls in the oil and fry, turning occasionally, for 4 to 5 minutes, or until golden. Transfer the rice balls to the prepared plate, cover with aluminum foil and keep warm in the oven heated to the lowest setting. Repeat until all the rice balls have been fried. **11.** Spoon the aioli across a serving plate and top with the hot arancini.

Brunch

SERVES 4

1 lb (450 g) live mussels

½ cup (125 mL) unsalted butter, softened, divided

2 cups (500 mL) chanterelle mushrooms, lightly brushed clean

1 Tbsp (15 mL) fresh thyme leaves, plus extra for garnish

4 slices thick multigrain bread

4 tsp (20 mL) grainy mustard, divided

Freshly ground black pepper

½ cup (125 mL) Parmigiano-Reggiano cheese, grated, for garnish

MUSSELS & MUSHROOMS ON TOAST

I personally love toast because it works so great as a base or vessel. This dish reminds me of fall in Canada with the fresh thyme, browning butter, and earthiness of the mushrooms. Grab a glass of red wine like a nice pinot noir, sit back, and enjoy.

1. Clean the mussels under cold, running water. Remove any hair connected to the mussels and discard any mussels that are completely or even slightly open. Set aside. 2. In a large skillet or medium-size saucepan over medium-high heat, place 1 to 2 cups (250 to 500 mL) of cold water and bring it to a boil. Place the mussels in the saucepan, cover, and steam for 2 to 3 minutes, or until most of them have opened. Transfer the mussels and their juice into a large bowl. Discard any mussels that did not open. Once the mussels have cooled, grip the top shell in one hand and the bottom shell in the other hand, and give a small pull to detach the shells. Using your fingers or a small fork, remove the meat from the shell and place it in a small bowl. Repeat with the remaining mussels and set aside. 3. In a separate skillet, melt half of the butter over medium heat. Add the mushrooms and fresh thyme, and cook for 1 to 2 minutes, until the mushrooms turn slightly brown. Add the mussel meats, stirring occasionally, and cook for 2 to 3 minutes, or until the liquid has reduced by at least half. 4. In the meantime, toast the bread. Spread each slice with the remaining butter and 1 tsp (5 mL) of the mustard. Spoon a generous portion of the mussel meat mixture onto each slice of toast. Top with pepper, some grated cheese and the remaining thyme leaves. 5. Serve immediately so that the toast doesn't get soggy.

Celeb Chef

SERVES 6

Smoked Mussels

2 lb (900 g) mussels

1 Tbsp (15 mL) salted butter

1 medium yellow onion, sliced

1 clove garlic, chopped

1 cup (250 mL) dry white wine

Wood chips, for smoking

1 tsp (5 mL) cold-pressed
   canola oil, for garnish

MAKES 9–12 ROLLS

Rolls

¼ cup + 1 Tbsp (75 mL)
   unsalted butter, plus extra
   melted butter for brushing

1 cup (250 mL) whole milk

¼ cup (75 mL) granulated
   sugar

1 ½ tsp (7 mL) dry active yeast

4 cups (1 L) all-purpose flour

1 tsp (5 mL) kosher salt

1 egg, beaten, mixed with
   milk, for egg wash

SMOKED MUSSELS WITH BUTTER ROLLS & WHIPPED CREAM CHEESE BY CHARLOTTE LANGLEY

Smoked and otherwise preserved shellfish have been a part of my life for as long as I can remember. I grew up in PEI, where a big part of our community culture was preserving fish and shellfish in a variety of ways to keep our larders stocked all winter. Matt came to me a few years ago when I was working at a fish shop and started chatting with me, talking a mile a minute, about fish, and distribution, and a whole bunch of other things. To be honest, I was a little taken aback by his quick banter! But when I finally had the opportunity to get involved in the conversation, I quickly realized that we had a mutual love for the ocean and that we might even be cousins! I am seriously flattered to have been asked to be a part of this book, and I hope you enjoy these traditional flavors with a modern touch.

1. Clean the mussels under cold, running water. Remove any hair connected to the mussels and discard any mussels that are completely or even slightly open. Set aside in the fridge. 2. In a large saucepan over medium heat, melt the butter. Sweat the onions and garlic in the butter until the onions have turned translucent and the garlic is fragrant, about 5 to 8 minutes. 3. Throw the mussels in the saucepan and deglaze the pan with the white wine. Cover the saucepan with a tight-fitting lid and steam the mussels until just cooked, 2 to 3 minutes, or until they start to open. 4. Using a slotted spoon, transfer the mussels to a large bowl, discarding any that did not open. Reserve the steaming liquid. 5. Once the mussels have cooled, grip the top shell in one hand and the bottom shell in the other hand, and give a small pull to detach the shells. Using your fingers or a small fork, remove the meat from the shell and place it in a small bowl. Repeat with the remaining mussels and set them aside in a perforated pan or metal colander. 6. Meanwhile, start a fire in your backyard with charcoal and paper or preheat your barbecue to 350°F (180°C). Throw some small pieces of wood on top of the fire or in a smoke maze on the barbecue and place the colander of mussels on top of the smoky fire for 10 to 15 minutes. You're looking for a subtle smoke. 7. To serve, gently place the mussels in a small mason jar and pour some of the reserved steaming liquid overtop. Drizzle with the canola oil, or any other mild-tasting oil, and eat with the super-soft butter rolls and whipped cream cheese.

Whipped Cream Cheese

2 cups (500 mL) full-fat cream cheese, at room temperature

1 ½ tsp (7 mL) fennel seeds, measured, toasted, and ground

1 ½ tsp (7 mL) black peppercorns, measured, toasted, and ground

Kosher salt, to taste

CHARLOTTE'S BUTTER ROLLS & WHIPPED CREAM CHEESE

1. In a small saucepan, melt the butter in the milk over low heat. Remove from the heat and allow to cool until it's the temperature of your skin. 2. Transfer the milk-butter mixture to a large bowl or the bowl of your stand mixer fitted with a pastry hook. Add the sugar and yeast to the milk and let it bloom—it will look fluffy and bubbly, and it should take between 5 and 10 minutes. 3. Add the flour and salt, and mix on medium-low speed until the dough is well formed and is coming away from the sides of the bowl, about 7 to 10 minutes. Don't rush this step. 4. Remove the bowl from the stand mixer, cover with a clean, damp dish towel, and let the dough rise in a moderately warm, draft-free place for 1 hour. 5. Once the dough has risen, remove it from the bowl and punch it down. 6. Divide the dough into about 9 to 12 pieces, each ¼ cup (60 mL) in size, and shape them into individual balls as smooth as you can make them. Place the rolls on a baking tray lined with parchment paper. 7. Cover the rolls again with the dish towel and let sit in the same warm spot for about 30 minutes. 8. Meanwhile, place the cream cheese, fennel seeds, and black peppercorns in a large bowl. Whip with a hand-held mixer or mix with a wooden spoon. 9. Preheat the oven to 350°F (180°C). 10. Once the buns have risen again, brush the tops with the egg wash and bake until golden, 12 to 15 minutes. Remove the buns from the oven and brush with the melted butter for a soft, delicious crust. 11. To serve, open up a warm bun and spread it generously with the whipped cream cheese. Top with a few smoked mussels and enjoy!

OCTOPUS & SQUID

SERVES 4–8

1 frozen octopus
(2–3 lb/900 g–1.3 kg),
thawed

2 cloves garlic, minced

1 small jalapeño, seeded and
finely diced

½ cup (125 mL) finely
chopped red onion

½ cup (125 mL) finely
chopped cilantro

1 tsp (5 mL) chili powder

½ tsp (2 mL) kosher salt

Juice from 1 lime

1 medium avocado

8 tostada shells (or deep-fried
corn tortillas)

1 Tbsp (15 mL) smoked
paprika

½ cup (125 mL) crumbled
queso fresco cheese or feta
cheese

BEACHSIDE TOSTADAS

There is absolutely nothing better than crunchy, fresh tostadas—especially when they're made with corn tortillas. I recently came back from a friend's wedding in Tulum, Mexico, where I enjoyed some of the most amazing tostadas I've ever eaten. Tip back a couple of mezcals and you have a party! I like to eat my tostadas warm, so when they come out of the oil, I season them with salt and top them with the chilled octopus mixture right away. Delicious!

1. To prepare the octopus, using a sharp kitchen knife, remove the tentacles by holding up each individual tentacle and cutting it off at the head. A frozen octopus will already have been cleaned of its sac and innards. Discard the head. 2. Bring a large stockpot filled with 8 cups (2 L) of cold water to a boil over high heat. Carefully place the tentacles in the boiling water and cook, covered, for 10 to 12 minutes. To test if the tentacles are ready, pierce them with a knife. If the knife slides in easily, the tentacles are cooked. If they're not ready, keep them in for another 2 to 5 minutes then test again. Be careful not to overcook the tentacles. Drain the tentacles and then chop them into ½-inch (1.2 cm) pieces. 3. Place the octopus pieces in a large mixing bowl. Add the garlic, jalapeño, red onions, cilantro, chili powder, salt, and lime juice. Mix well to combine. Cover with plastic wrap and refrigerate for 30 to 45 minutes to allow the flavors to come together. 4. Cut the avocado into ¼-inch (6 mm) cubes. 5. To serve, take each tostada and sprinkle it with paprika. Top evenly with the octopus mixture, avocado cubes, and crumbled cheese.

Dinner

SERVES 2–4

1 fresh octopus
   (2–3 lb/900 g–1.3 kg)

2 large shallots, finely diced

2 sprigs fresh tarragon

1 lb (450 g) new potatoes

½ cup (125 mL) black olive
   paste or tapenade

Kosher salt and freshly ground
   black pepper

2 Tbsp (30 mL) Spanish
   paprika (also known as
   Pimentón)

Extra-virgin olive oil, to drizzle

Lemon Caper Dip (page 225)

NOTE: When boiling the
octopus, add a few wine
corks to the liquid to help
the tentacles tenderize.
According to the old wives'
tale, the cork's natural
enzymes help this process
along. I swear by it!

TORREMOLINOS OCTOPUS

This recipe was inspired by my travels to Torremolinos, Spain. I admired its white, sandy beaches and loved the hot Mediterranean sun, and when the locals told me that it's sunny there 364 days a year, I found myself wondering why I live in Canada, where it's winter for much of the year. One of the best parts of visiting the Costa del Sol—the southern part of Spain—was that almost every restaurant served some kind of octopus dish. I loved sitting in the restaurants late at night (locals don't go for dinner until 10:00 p.m. or later), people watching and eating beautifully prepared tapas such as this one.

1. If your fishmonger hasn't cleaned your octopus for you, you'll want to do that before you get started. Start by cutting the head in half—you'll see the ink sac and innards. Carefully cut these out and discard them. You can either fully remove the head or not; it's a matter of preference. Flip the octopus upside down—you'll see the entry to the beak. Simply push it up from underneath and it will easily pop out. You're all set to cook! 2. Fill a saucepan large enough to hold the octopus with cold water and bring it to a boil over high heat. Add the octopus, shallots, and tarragon. Boil the octopus, uncovered, for 30 minutes. Add the potatoes and cook for another 20 to 30 minutes, or until both the octopus and potatoes are tender. To test if the octopus's tentacles are ready, pierce them with a knife. If the knife slides in easily, they're ready. If they're not ready, cook for another 2 to 5 minutes, but be careful not to overcook. 3. Carefully remove the octopus from the water. Place it in a large bowl and allow to cool at room temperature until you can comfortably handle it. 4. Remove the potatoes from the saucepan, being careful that they don't break, and place them in a separate bowl. Allow them to cool at room temperature and then slice them in half. 5. Once the octopus is cool, cut the tentacles from the head (if you haven't discarded the head already) and slice them into ½-inch (1.2 cm) pieces. 6. Spread the black olive tapenade on a large serving platter, and arrange the tentacle pieces and potatoes on top. Season with salt and pepper to taste. Garnish with paprika and a drizzle of extra-virgin olive oil. Serve with a side of Lemon Caper Dip. This dish can be eaten chilled or hot.

Brunch

GRILLED OCTOPUS & ITALIAN SPICY SAUSAGE

SERVES 2–4

1 fresh octopus
(2–3 lb/900 g–1.3 kg)

1 lemon

¼ cup (60 mL) extra-virgin
olive oil

2 Tbsp (30 mL) dried oregano

2 Tbsp (30 mL) dried rosemary

2 Tbsp (30 mL) dried thyme

4 large spicy Italian sausages

Kosher salt and freshly ground
black pepper

1 Tbsp (15 mL) ground cumin

One of my favorite ways to prepare octopus is to grill it. Grilling octopus adds some delicious smokiness, and I love the crisp char it gets. The Italian sausage in this dish adds just the right amount of heat. I hope you enjoy this dish as much as I do. (I like to serve it with Matty's BBQ'd Mexican Street Corn [page 193].)

1. If your fishmonger hasn't cleaned your octopus for you, you'll want to do that before you get started. Start by cutting the head in half—you'll see the ink sac and innards. Carefully cut these out and discard them. You can either fully remove the head or not; it's a matter of preference. Flip the octopus upside down—you'll see the entry to the beak. Simply push it up from underneath and it will easily pop out. Slice the lemon in half widthwise. Zest and juice one half; set the other half aside for the garnish. 2. Place the octopus in a large bowl, add the lemon juice and zest, olive oil, oregano, rosemary, and thyme and mix to combine. Cover with plastic wrap, and marinate, refrigerated, for 1 to 2 hours. 3. Preheat the grill to 375°F (190°C). Using a paper towel with a little bit of extra-virgin olive oil on it, wipe the grill so that the octopus won't stick. 4. Lay the octopus on the preheated grill, being careful that the tentacles do not fall through the grates. Cook the octopus, flipping once, for 10 to 12 minutes, or until it's charred with grill marks and tender. To test if the octopus is ready, pierce a tentacle with a knife. If the knife slides in easily, it's ready. If it's not ready, let it cook for another 2 to 3 minutes, but be careful not to overcook. 5. While the octopus cooks, grill the sausages for 5 to 8 minutes on each side, or until the juices run clear when you prick a sausage with a knife. Grill the remaining lemon half for 1 to 2 minutes, or until charred. 6. Remove the octopus and sausages from the grill. Lay the sausages on a serving board or plate. Place the grilled octopus on top of the bed of sausages and season to taste with salt and pepper. Garnish with the ground cumin and serve with your favorite side dish.

Lunch

SERVES 2–4

2 Tbsp (30 mL) canola oil

4–6 octopus tentacles (see note on page 118)

2 cups (500 mL) extra-virgin olive oil

2 cloves garlic, crushed

2 tsp (10 mL) sweet paprika

2 tsp (10 mL) ground harissa

2 tsp (10 mL) ground cumin

Juice from 1 lemon

1 bunch cilantro, finely chopped

2 cups (500 mL) couscous

1 bunch mint, leaves only, for garnish

¼ cup (60 mL) pomegranate seeds, for garnish

¼ cup (60 mL) toasted sliced almonds, for garnish

OLIVE OIL–POACHED MOROCCAN OCTOPUS

If you've ever been to Morocco you'll know they have some delicious fresh octopus, and I must say, the depth of flavors that they create in their dishes is beyond anything I've ever had anywhere else. I had the opportunity to live in a *riad*, a traditional Moroccan house with a courtyard, for two weeks while visiting Marrakesh. The owners of the *riad* were serious cooks and introduced me to some great ingredients and traditional Moroccan cooking techniques that will always stay with me.

1. In a large sauté pan, heat the canola oil over high heat. Sear each side of the octopus tentacles for about 30 seconds, or until slightly crisp and brown on the outside. Quickly remove them from the pan. 2. In a large saucepan, bring the extra-virgin olive oil to a simmer over medium heat—the oil is ready when it shimmers. Add the seared tentacles and poach for 20 to 25 minutes, flipping once. Watch them carefully, and test them at the 20-minute mark so you don't overcook them. To test to if the octopus is ready, pierce a tentacle with a knife. If the knife slides in easily, it's ready. 3. In a medium-size mixing bowl, combine the garlic, paprika, harissa, and cumin with the lemon juice. Add the chopped cilantro and mix well. Set aside at room temperature. 4. To prepare the couscous, in a large saucepan over high heat, bring 3 cups (750 mL) of cold water to a boil. Add the couscous, stir once with a spoon, and turn off the heat. Steam, covered, for 5 to 7 minutes, or until all the water has been incorporated and the couscous has absorbed the water. Fluff the couscous with a fork just before serving. 5. In a large saucepan, warm the paprika mixture over medium-high heat. Add the poached tentacles and cook for 1 to 2 minutes, just to warm them through. 6. Create a bed of cooked couscous on each serving plate. Top with octopus tentacles and sauce. Garnish with the mint leaves, pomegranate seeds, and almonds.

Quick & Easy

SERVES 2

½ cup (125 mL) soy sauce

½ cup (125 mL) yuzu juice (find this at an Asian specialty food store)

1 Tbsp (15 mL) Sriracha hot sauce

2 raw octopus tentacles (see note)

2 Tbsp (30 mL) black seaweed kelp caviar (find this at an Asian specialty food store)

2 green onions, thinly sliced

NOTE: Most fishmongers will sell you individual octopus tentacles, or you can buy a whole octopus and section it yourself. You can also replace the kelp caviar with any caviar you prefer.

OCTOPUS CARPACCIO WITH SPICY PONZU SAUCE

I always serve this dish on cold plates, as I think it helps to keep the temperature of the octopus perfect. Technique and patience are the keys to success with this dish. Okay, so maybe one more—make sure you have a very sharp knife to cut the octopus. I had the excitement of buying a Gyuto chef's knife when I was in Japan. The Gyuto family has been making knives for hundreds of years. It's a fantastic knife and, with the right care and maintenance, it will last for a lifetime.

1. In a large mixing bowl, combine the soy sauce, yuzu juice, and Sriracha hot sauce to make the spicy ponzu sauce. Mix well, cover, and place in the refrigerator.
2. Using a sharp knife, carefully cut the octopus tentacles on the bias into very thin pieces, about ¼-inch (6 mm) thick. Divide the octopus slices between two serving plates with high rims. Cover with plastic wrap and refrigerate for 30 to 45 minutes.
3. Remove the plates from the refrigerator and carefully pour equal amounts of the ponzu sauce along the outside edges of the plate, without fully submerging the octopus in the sauce. 4. Using a teaspoon, place a small amount of the kelp caviar in the middle of each piece of octopus. Garnish with green onion slices.

Lunch

SERVES 2–4

2 fresh large squids, about ½ lb (225 g) each

½ lb (225 g) whole, raw shrimp

1 Tbsp (15 mL) grated fresh ginger

1 Tbsp (15 mL) garlic powder

1 egg yolk

Kosher salt and freshly ground black pepper

2 Tbsp (30 mL) sesame oil

1 cup (250 mL) cornstarch

1 cup (250 mL) canola oil

8 cups (2 L) chicken stock

1 tsp (5 mL) fish sauce

1 Tbsp (15 mL) soy sauce

1 Tbsp (15 mL) Sriracha hot sauce

2 green onions, finely sliced, for garnish

JAPANESE STREET FOOD SQUID BALL SOUP

This soup may sound quirky but it's packed with flavor and protein. It's a great soup for anyone with a busy day ahead of them, which is why I like it for lunch.

1. Clean each squid under cold, running water. Grasp the squid head above the eyes and pull it out of the mantle (the body) in one solid motion. The innards should mostly slide out as well. Then, using your fingers, reach into the mantle and pull out and discard any additional innards, including the piece of thick, clear cartilage. Gently scrape the outside of the mantle with a knife to remove the speckles of the squid, leaving only the white meat of the mantle. Cut the mantle into rings, and set the rings and tentacles aside. **2.** Using your thumb, pry the shells off each shrimp. Devein them by using a paring knife to cut a shallow slit from head to tail. Then, using the knife tip, carefully remove the black vein and discard it. Remove the heads of the shrimp. Rough chop the shrimp. **3.** In a food processor fitted with the steel blade, place the squid meat, shrimp, ginger, garlic powder, egg yolk, and a pinch each of salt and pepper. Add the sesame oil and process to a smooth paste. Place the mixture in a bowl, cover with plastic wrap, and refrigerate for 1 hour to set. **4.** Remove the mixture from the refrigerator. Using a tablespoon for even balls, form fish balls with your hands about 1 inch (2.5 cm) in diameter. Place the balls on a plate and refrigerate, uncovered, for 10 to 15 minutes. **5.** Line a baking tray with parchment paper. Line a plate with paper towels. **6.** Place the cornstarch in a medium-size mixing bowl and dredge the balls, shaking off any excess cornstarch. Place the coated balls on the prepared baking tray. **7.** In a medium-size saucepan, heat the canola oil to 350°F (180°C). Check the temperature with a cooking thermometer. **8.** Working in small batches and using a metal slotted spoon, place the balls in the hot oil for 2 to 3 minutes, or until crispy and brown. Move them around as they cook so they brown evenly. Using the slotted spoon, transfer them to the prepared plate to absorb any excess oil. Make sure the oil comes back to temperature in between batches. **9.** In a separate large saucepan, combine the chicken stock, fish sauce, soy sauce, and Sriracha hot sauce over medium-high heat. Bring to a simmer, stirring occasionally. Carefully place the fried balls in the stock, bring the soup to a boil, and cook for 3 to 5 minutes. Season to taste with salt and pepper. **10.** As soon as the balls are warm, ladle the soup into bowls, garnish with the green onions, and enjoy.

CRISPY SQUID WITH TAHINI DRESSING

SERVES 2–4

2 fresh large squids, about ½ lb (225 g) each

2 cloves garlic, minced

½ cup (125 mL) tahini, plus more for serving

2 Tbsp (30 mL) finely chopped dill

1 Tbsp (15 mL) honey

½ tsp (2 mL) ground turmeric

2 Tbsp (30 mL) olive oil

Juice and zest from 1 lemon

Juice from ¼ orange

1 cup (250 mL) all-purpose flour

1 tsp (5 mL) kosher salt

2 large eggs

1 cup (250 mL) Italian breadcrumbs

1 cup (250 mL) canola oil

1 Tbsp (15 mL) ground sumac, for garnish

The flavor profiles in this dish remind me of my travels to Morocco. The fragrant spices and fresh aromatics make for a memorable pairing. Combine those with a little bit of crunch and you have the basis for the perfect recipe. I like to use canola oil to fry most of my foods because it's a neutral oil, which means it doesn't add any extra unwanted flavor. It also has one of the highest smoke points of all the oils—that's key to the success of this recipe, because you don't want it to burn.

1. Clean each squid under cold, running water. Grasp the squid head above the eyes and pull it out of the mantle (the body) in one solid motion. The innards should mostly slide out as well. Then, using your fingers, reach into the mantle and pull out and discard any additional innards, including the piece of thick, clear cartilage. Gently scrape the outside of the mantle with a knife to remove the speckles of the squid, leaving only the white meat of the mantle. Cut the mantle into ¼- to ½-inch-thick (6 mm to 1.2 cm) rings and save the tentacles for another recipe—the tentacles will keep in the fridge, covered, for 2 to 3 days. Set the rings aside in the fridge until needed. 2. In a food processor fitted with the steel blade, place the garlic, tahini, dill, honey, and turmeric. Pulse to combine. As you do so, slowly add the olive oil, lemon juice and zest, and orange juice. Transfer the sauce to a bowl, cover, and refrigerate until needed. 3. Set up a dredging station by placing the flour and salt in one large bowl, beating the eggs in another bowl, and placing the breadcrumbs in a third bowl. Line a baking tray with parchment paper. 4. Dredge the squid rings in the flour, then in the egg wash, and then in the breadcrumbs, coating evenly at each step and shaking gently to remove any excess breadcrumbs. Set the prepared squid rings on the prepared baking tray. 5. In a medium-size saucepan, heat the canola oil over medium-high heat to 350–375°F (180–190°C). Use a cooking thermometer to check the temperature. Line a plate with paper towels. 6. Working in small batches, fry the rings for 1 to 2 minutes, or until they turn crispy and golden brown. Using tongs, remove the rings from the oil and place them on the prepared plate to absorb any excess oil. Repeat the process until all the rings have been fried, making sure that the oil comes back up to temperature in between batches. 7. To serve, place the rings in a large bowl, spoon the tahini sauce overtop, and sprinkle with sumac.

Dinner

SERVES 2–4

4 fresh small squids, about
¾ lb (340 g) each

1 Tbsp (15 mL) canola oil

1 Tbsp (15 mL) sesame oil

4 green onions, finely chopped

2 cloves garlic, finely chopped

2 thinly diced red Thai chilies,
plus extra for garnish

1 stalk lemongrass, finely
chopped

¼ cup (60 mL) finely chopped
cilantro

1 Tbsp (15 mL) finely chopped
fresh ginger

2 Tbsp (30 mL) soy sauce

1 tsp (5 mL) fish sauce

LATE-NIGHT CHINESE SQUID

So simple, so clean, and so good! It's easy to see why dishes like this one can be found in tons of late-night street food stalls all over the world. While I was in Asia, I noticed that squid seemed to be an ingredient in almost everything, but this late-night adaptation has stayed in my memory for years.

1. Clean each squid under cold, running water. Grasp the squid head above the eyes and pull it out of the mantle (the body) in one solid motion. The innards should mostly slide out as well. Then, using your fingers, reach into the mantle and pull out and discard any additional innards, including the piece of thick, clear cartilage. Gently scrape the outside of the mantle with a knife to remove the speckles of the squid, leaving the white meat of the mantle. Cut the mantle into ¼- to ½-inch-thick (6 mm to 1.2 cm) rings. **2.** In a large wok or sauté pan, heat the oils together over medium-high heat. Make sure you turn on your stovetop fan, as this dish can get a bit smoky. Once the oils are shimmering, stir-fry the squid rings and tentacles, continuously stirring, for 2 to 3 minutes. The key to a good stir-fry is to keep the ingredients constantly moving so that they don't burn over the high heat. Add 3 Tbsp (45 mL) of cold water, the green onions, garlic, chilies, lemongrass, cilantro, ginger, soy sauce, and fish sauce. Continue to stir-fry for 1 to 2 minutes, or until the flavors are combined. **3.** Serve this dish on a bed of rice to make it a main dish or on small side plates for the perfect appetizer. Garnish with thin slices of red chilies.

Dinner

SQUID INK-BAKED MANICOTTI

SERVES 4

8 uncooked manicotti shells

2 Tbsp (30 mL) squid ink (see note on page 95)

1 Tbsp (15 mL) canola oil

1 cup (250 mL) finely chopped white onion

4 cloves garlic, finely diced

1 Tbsp (15 mL) chili flakes

1½ cups (375 mL) tomato sauce

Kosher salt and freshly ground black pepper

2 cups (500 mL) ricotta cheese

Freshly grated Parmigiano-Reggiano cheese, for garnish

8–12 small basil leaves, for garnish

What a great dish to eat with your eyes first. This is a meal that is sure to impress any guests you may have over for dinner. It's unique, it's interesting, and it's freakin' delicious. I remember when I was about 16 years old, the chef at the Boatworks restaurant where I was working used squid ink and I thought it was so cool. Have fun with the squid ink. It's blue-black in color and like no other ingredient you have probably used before. It's time to try something new!

1. Preheat the oven to 375°F (190°C). **2.** Fill a medium-size saucepan with 8 cups (2 L) of cold, salted water and bring it to a boil over high heat. Cook the manicotti shells for 2 to 3 minutes, keeping them al dente. Drain the water. Add the squid ink to the manicotti and gently toss to coat them, being careful not to break the shells. Set aside. **3.** In a medium-size sauté pan over medium heat, place the canola oil, onions, garlic, and chili flakes. Cook for 2 to 3 minutes, stirring frequently, or until the onions are soft. Add the tomato sauce and simmer for 1 to 2 minutes to allow the flavors to combine. Season to taste with salt and pepper. Remove from the heat. **4.** Place the ricotta cheese in a piping bag fitted with a small round tip, or in a resealable plastic bag with one of the corners cut off. Evenly pipe the ricotta cheese into the black pasta shells. **5.** In a 13- x 9-inch (33 x 23 cm) baking dish, spread one-quarter of the tomato sauce. Place the stuffed manicotti on top. Pour over the remaining tomato sauce. Bake, uncovered, for 15 to 20 minutes, or until hot and bubbling. **6.** Garnish with the Parmigiano-Reggiano and basil leaves.

Party!

FRIED SQUID PINTXO POPPERS

SERVES 2–4

4 fresh small squids, about ¾ lb (340 g) each

8 small Padrón peppers, or 2 green bell peppers cut in large pieces

1 fresh medium piquillo pepper

2 large eggs

Juice from ½ lemon

1 cup (250 mL) extra-virgin olive oil

1 tsp (5 mL) smoked paprika

Kosher salt and freshly ground black pepper

1 cup (250 mL) corn flour

2 large eggs, beaten

1 cup (250 mL) Panko breadcrumbs

1½ cups (375 mL) canola oil

1 Tbsp (15 mL) flaky sea salt

Special equipment

4 cocktail skewers, about 6–8 inches (15–20 cm) long

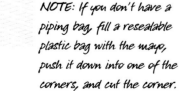

NOTE: If you don't have a piping bag, fill a resealable plastic bag with the mayo, push it down into one of the corners, and cut the corner.

Vinup is one of my favorite tapas bars in Spain. It has rows and rows of pintxos by the entrance so you see them when you walk in. You choose all these great hand-held snacks, and pair them with samples of Spanish wines. How wonderful does that sound?

1. Preheat the oven to 375°F (190°C). 2. Clean each squid under cold, running water. Grasp the squid head above the eyes and pull it out of the mantle (the body) in one solid motion. The innards should mostly slide out as well. Then, using your fingers, reach into the mantle and pull out and discard any additional innards, including the piece of thick, clear cartilage. Gently scrape the outside of the mantle with a knife to remove the speckles of the squid, leaving only the white meat of the mantle. Keep the squid whole and set aside in the fridge until needed. Use the tentacles for another recipe. They will keep in the fridge, covered, for 2 to 3 days. 3. Place the Padrón and piquillo peppers on a baking tray and roast in the oven for 15 to 18 minutes, or until blackened and soft. Remove any blackened or charred bits from the skins. Separate the piquillo pepper from the Padrón and set aside. 4. In a food processor fitted with the steel blade, blend the eggs and lemon juice. Slowly add the olive oil in a continuous stream while the food processor is running. Once the mayo is emulsified, add the paprika and then kosher salt and pepper to taste. Combine well. Add the piquillo pepper and blend fully. Transfer the pepper mayo to a piping bag fitted with a small round tip, or a resealable plastic bag (see note) and set in the fridge to cool. 5. Set up a dredging station by placing the corn flour in one bowl, beating the eggs in another bowl, and placing the breadcrumbs in a third bowl. 6. In a large saucepan, heat the canola oil to 350–375°F (180–190°C). Use a cooking thermometer to check the temperature. Line a plate with paper towels. 7. Dredge the squids in the flour, then the eggs, and then the breadcrumbs, coating evenly at each step and shaking gently to remove any excess breadcrumbs. 8. Using tongs, carefully lay the coated squids in the hot oil and fry for 2 to 3 minutes, or until golden brown. Using tongs, transfer the squids to the prepared plate to absorb any excess oil and cool completely. 9. Using the piping bag, pipe the pepper mayo into each of the hollow fried squids. 10. Skewer a Padrón pepper then a squid, followed by another Padrón pepper. Sprinkle with flaky sea salt. Repeat the process until all the squids are skewered, and serve, with any leftover pepper mayo.

OYSTERS

Party!

SERVES 16

12 oysters

½ lb (225 g) chorizo sausage

2 Tbsp (30 mL) unsalted butter

4 cloves garlic, finely minced

½ cup (125 mL) finely minced shallots

¼ cup (60 mL) dry white wine

Kosher salt and freshly ground black pepper

½ cup (125 mL) Italian breadcrumbs

¼ cup (60 mL) fresh sage leaves

16 large Portobello mushrooms, cleaned, trimmed, and stems and gills discarded

¾ cup (175 mL) grated Pecorino cheese

CHORIZO & OYSTER-STUFFED MUSHROOMS

This recipe was inspired by one of my trips to Spain and is perfect for parties, which I love. I have to admit that stuffed mushrooms caps were one of my favorite snacks as a child. Consider this a "big kids" version. I love chorizo here, but feel free to replace it with any other meat that you prefer. Seasoned ground beef would also work well in this dish.

1. Preheat the oven to 375°F (190°C). 2. Using a brush or a clean steel wool pad, scrub the grit from each of the oyster shells and rinse them under cold, running water. Grasp an oyster in one hand, cup-side down, insert an oyster knife into the opening, and run it from top to bottom of the hinge, which should open it. If the hinge doesn't open, try giving the knife a small twist in the center of the hinge. Using your fingers, remove the top shell of each oyster. Slip the knife under the oyster meat to loosen the lower adductors, allowing you to remove the meat and discard the liquor. Gently clean off any dark parts around the oyster meat. Finely chop the meat. You should have about 1 cup (250 mL) of meat. Discard the shells. 3. Remove the chorizo meat from its casing and use your fingers to finely crumble the meat. 4. In large sauté pan, melt the butter over medium-high heat. Add the oyster meat, chorizo, garlic, shallots, and wine and sauté, stirring, for 4 to 5 minutes. Season to taste with salt and pepper. Turn down the heat to medium and then add the breadcrumbs and sage. Stir well, allow to simmer for a couple of minutes, then remove the pan from the heat. 5. On a large baking tray, place an even layer of the hollow mushrooms caps. Spoon about 1 Tbsp (15 mL) of the oyster mixture into each of the mushrooms caps, sprinkle with cheese, and bake for 8 to 10 minutes, or until the cheese is fully melted and golden brown. 6. Remove the mushroom caps from the oven and serve immediately.

party!

SERVES 6–8

½ cup (125 mL) uncooked thick-cut strip bacon, chopped into ½-inch (1.2 cm) cubes

1 cup (250 mL) unsalted butter, at room temperature

½ cup (125 mL) shredded aged cheddar cheese

¼ cup (60 mL) finely chopped flat-leaf parsley

1 Tbsp (15 mL) Worcestershire sauce

1 Tbsp (15 mL) hot sauce

1 tsp (5 mL) sweet paprika

24 fresh oysters

BACON & CHEESE OYSTERS

This recipe combines three of my favorite ingredients—bacon, cheese, and, of course, oysters. This is the perfect recipe for any summer BBQ party. Next time you hit the beach with your mini grill and cooler, consider trying this dish out.

1. Preheat the barbecue to 375°F (190°C). **2.** In a food processor fitted with the steel blade, place the bacon, butter, cheese, parsley, Worcestershire sauce, hot sauce, and paprika. Process until mixed well. Set aside. **3.** Using a brush or a clean steel wool pad, scrub the grit from each of the oyster shells and rinse them under cold, running water. Grasp an oyster in one hand, cup-side down, insert an oyster knife into the opening, and run it from top to bottom of the hinge, which should open it. If the hinge doesn't open, try giving the knife a small twist in the center of the hinge. Using your fingers, remove the top shell of each oyster, leaving the meat in the shell. Gently clean off any dark parts around the oyster meat. Carefully slide the knife between the meat and the shell to separate the meat from the adductors. Discard the top shells. **4.** Place the oysters, shell side down, directly onto the preheated grill of the barbecue. Spoon about 1 Tbsp (15 mL) of the bacon mixture into each oyster. Cook, with the barbecue lid down, for 5 to 7 minutes, or until the oysters are golden brown and slightly crispy. **5.** Remove the oysters from the barbecue and serve immediately.

SERVES 2–4

12 oysters

1 cup (250 mL) buttermilk

½ cup (125 mL) all-purpose flour

1 cup (250 mL) Italian breadcrumbs

2 large eggs

2 Tbsp (30 mL) Cajun seasoning

2 cups (500 mL) canola oil

Kosher salt and freshly ground black pepper

CHICKEN-FRIED OYSTERS

"Buttermilk," "fried," and "oysters" are three words that will always bring a smile to my face. I love my country music and this recipe makes me think of my man, Zac Brown, rocking this tune: "You know I like my chicken fried, and cold beer on a Friday night." Something about fried chicken feels so relaxing to me. Just imagine washing this dish down with some sweet tea. As my friends in the USA know, chicken-fried steak with hot gravy is where it's at. Now switch out the steak and try this fun, new option from the sea.

1. Using a brush or a clean steel wool pad, scrub the grit from each of the oyster shells and rinse them under cold, running water. Grasp an oyster in one hand, cup-side down, insert an oyster knife into the opening, and run it from top to bottom of the hinge, which should open it. If the hinge doesn't open, try giving the knife a small twist in the center of the hinge. Using your fingers, remove the top shell of each oyster. Carefully slip the knife under the oyster meat to loosen the lower adductors, allowing you to remove the meat and discard the liquor. Gently clean off any dark parts around the oyster meat. Discard the shells. 2. Place the buttermilk in a small bowl along with the shucked oysters. Refrigerate, covered, for 2 to 3 hours to marinate. 3. Make a dredging station by placing the flour in one small bowl, the breadcrumbs in another small bowl, and whisking the eggs with the Cajun seasoning in a third small bowl. 4. Dredge each of the oyster meats, one at a time, in the flour, and then the egg wash, and then roll them in the breadcrumbs. Place the battered oysters on a baking tray. 5. In a large saucepan, heat the canola oil to 350°F (180°C). Use a cooking thermometer to check the temperature. Line a plate with paper towels. 6. Fry the oysters, in small batches to avoid overcrowding the pan, for 1 to 2 minutes, or until golden brown. Transfer them to the prepared plate to absorb any excess oil. Make sure to allow the oil to come back up to temperature in between batches. 7. Transfer the fried oysters to a serving plate. Season with salt and pepper to taste. 8. Serve warm with a dipping sauce. Try my Lemon Caper Dip (page 225) or Sriracha Mayo (page 226).

Lunch

SERVES 2

12 oysters (see note)

4 Tbsp (60 mL) full-fat mayonnaise

1 Tbsp (15 mL) Sriracha hot sauce

Kosher salt and freshly ground black pepper

2 baguettes

¾ cup (175 mL) thinly sliced English cucumber (skin on)

¼ cup (60 mL) carrots, cut into matchstick pieces then measured

1 red Thai chili, thinly sliced

Finely chopped cilantro, for garnish

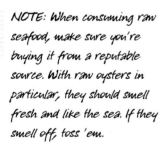

NOTE: When consuming raw seafood, make sure you're buying it from a reputable source. With raw oysters in particular, they should smell fresh and like the sea. If they smell off, toss 'em.

FRESH OYSTER BANH MI SANDWICH

Who doesn't love a good banh mi sandwich? Living in a multicultural city like Toronto, where we have a great Vietnamese community, I've had my fair share of these sandwiches. Simply put, it's a Vietnamese submarine sandwich loaded with a ton of flavor and great spices. Oysters aren't a traditional ingredient here, but I think they work perfectly.

1. Using a brush or a clean steel wool pad, scrub the grit from each of the oyster shells and rinse them under cold, running water. Grasp an oyster in one hand, cup-side down, insert an oyster knife into the opening, and run it from top to bottom of the hinge, which should open it. If the hinge doesn't open, try giving the knife a small twist in the center of the hinge. Using your fingers, remove the top shell of each oyster. Slip the knife under the oyster meat to loosen the lower adductors, allowing you to remove the meat and discard the liquor. Gently clean off any dark parts around the oyster meat. Set the oyster meat aside on a plate, uncovered, in the refrigerator. Discard the shells. 2. In a small bowl, mix together the mayonnaise and Sriracha hot sauce. Season to taste with salt and pepper. Set aside at room temperature. 3. Slice each baguette into two pieces, and then slice those pieces in half horizontally, to make small submarine sandwiches. 4. Lay out two bread bottoms and top each one with cucumber slices, carrots, and slices of chili. Top with the raw oyster meat, a drizzle of Sriracha mayo, and garnish of cilantro. Cover with the bread tops. Repeat for the second sandwich.

Party!

SERVES 24

48 medium oysters

1 ½ cups (375 mL) unsalted butter, softened

½ cup (125 mL) finely grated Parmigiano-Reggiano cheese

¼ cup (60 mL) finely chopped flat-leaf parsley

2 cloves garlic, minced

1 Tbsp (15 mL) Worcestershire sauce

1 tsp (5 mL) smoked paprika

½ tsp (2 mL) cayenne pepper

½ tsp (2 mL) hot sauce

GRILLED OYSTERS

I had the pleasure of traveling to Prince Edward Island for two summers and even hosted the Summerside Lobster Festival there. Both years, I had the honor of cooking with chefs from the local Mi'kmaq First Nation reserve. They made traditional grilled oysters from a recipe that has been passed down through many generations. They were delicious, and this is my take on that classic recipe.

1. Preheat the barbecue to 450°F (230°C). **2.** Using a brush or a clean steel wool pad, scrub the grit from each of the oyster shells and rinse them under cold, running water. Grasp an oyster in one hand, cup-side down, insert an oyster knife into the opening, and run it from top to bottom of the hinge, which should open it. If the hinge doesn't open, try giving the knife a small twist in the center of the hinge. Using your fingers, remove the top shell of each oyster. Slip the oyster knife under the oyster meat to loosen the lower adductors. Gently clean off any dark parts around the oyster meat. Set the oysters aside on a plate, uncovered, in the refrigerator. Discard the top shells. **3.** In a food processor fitted with the steel blade, place the butter, cheese, parsley, garlic, Worcestershire sauce, paprika, cayenne pepper, and hot sauce. Pulse until thoroughly mixed. **4.** Arrange the oysters, shell side down, in a single layer on the preheated grill. Spoon 1 Tbsp (15 mL) of the butter mixture into each oyster. Grill, uncovered, for 3 to 4 minutes, and then close the lid and grill for an additional 1 to 2 minutes, or until the edges of the oysters begin to curl. **5.** Transfer to a platter and serve immediately.

Brunch

WAKEY WAKEY OYSTERS BAKEY

SERVES 2–4

Oysters

12 oysters

3 cloves garlic, minced

¼ cup (60 mL) canola oil

½ cup (125 mL) Panko
breadcrumbs

½ cup (125 mL) grated
Parmigiano-Reggiano
cheese, divided

3 large egg yolks

2 Tbsp (30 mL) lemon juice

¼ tsp (1 mL) cayenne pepper

⅓ cup (75 mL) unsalted butter,
melted

Classic Mornay Sauce

¼ cup (60 mL) unsalted butter

¼ cup (60 mL) all-purpose flour

2 cups (500 mL) warm 2% milk

1 tsp (5 mL) ground cloves

Kosher salt and freshly ground
black pepper

¼ cup (60 mL) heavy (3.5%)
cream

1 cup (250 mL) grated
Emmental cheese

This simple dish is perfect for sleepy Sunday mornings. Hooray for breakfast in bed! Okay, so maybe you shouldn't actually eat this in bed, but I do know that you'll certainly feel relaxed and satisfied after you've finished eating it. I suggest serving this with hollandaise or Mornay sauce. Do you know the difference between the two? Hollandaise is a butter-based sauce and Mornay is a rich, creamy, cheese sauce. If you ask me, both are great, but Mornay takes the cake!

1. Preheat the oven to 375°F (190°C). **2.** Using a brush or a clean steel wool pad, scrub the grit from each of the oyster shells and rinse them under cold, running water. Grasp an oyster in one hand, cup-side down, insert an oyster knife into the opening, and run it from top to bottom of the hinge, which should open it. If the hinge doesn't open, try giving the knife a small twist in the center of the hinge. Using your fingers, remove the top shell of each oyster. Gently clean off any dark parts around the oyster meat. Slip the oyster knife under the oyster meat to loosen the lower adductors, allowing you to remove the meat and discard the liquor. Keep the meat intact and keep the bottom shells for baking. **3.** In a sauté pan over medium-low heat, sauté the garlic in the canola oil for 1 to 2 minutes, or until soft and fragrant. Remove from the heat and set aside at room temperature. **4.** Arrange the empty oyster shells on a baking tray. **5.** In a small bowl, place the cooked garlic, breadcrumbs, ¼ cup (60 mL) of the Parmigiano-Reggiano cheese, the egg yolks, lemon juice, and cayenne pepper. Pour the butter overtop and mix well to combine. **6.** Divide the breadcrumb mixture evenly between the oyster shells, packing it in tightly. Place a piece of oyster meat on top of the mixture and cover with the remaining Parmigiano-Reggiano cheese. **7.** Bake the oysters for 6 to 8 minutes, or until golden brown. **8.** Meanwhile, prepare the Mornay sauce. Melt the butter in a large saucepan over medium-high heat. Add the flour, stir together, and cook for approximately 1 minute, until a roux forms and the paste is a light golden brown. Slowly add the warm milk and continue to stir until the mixture is smooth and creamy. Add the cloves and a pinch each of salt and pepper. Stir to combine. Turn down the heat to low and stir in the heavy cream, until the mixture is thick enough to coat the back of a spoon. Add the Emmental cheese. Continue to stir until the cheese has completely melted. Remove the sauce from the heat. **9.** To serve, drizzle the oysters with the sauce. Enjoy immediately. If you have leftover sauce, it will keep covered in the fridge for 1 to 2 days.

Celeb Chef

SERVES 4

12 oysters

⅔ cup (150 mL) heavy (35%) cream

⅓ cup (75 mL) crumbled Stilton cheese

Scant ¼ cup (60 mL) good-quality port wine

Kosher salt and freshly ground black pepper

6 walnuts, finely chopped, for garnish

NOTE: The port wine gives this sauce its distinctive color.

JUSTICE LEAGUE OYSTERS
BY AFRIM PRISTINE

Matt Dean Pettit and I have been colleagues and friends for over seven years now, so when he called on me to submit a recipe for this cookbook, I not only felt honored, I also saw it as my heroic duty. You see, I absolutely adore superheroes and everything to do with them. In particular, I've loved Batman (for obvious reasons, because he's just so awesome) ever since my parents gave me my old school Adam West Batman cape when I was about 7 years old. Thirty years later, I still have that cape. If Matt Dean Pettit were a superhero (and I'm pretty sure he is), he would be Aquaman. No doubt, no question about it. MDP knows all about seafood and shellfish, and, like Aquaman, he can communicate with underwater creatures. In this recipe, Aquaman throws up the bat signal and I respond with a delicious cheesy and boozy oyster recipe. *WHAM! POW!* The English Stilton in this recipe is big and bold, with the perfect amount of salt and funk. I think it's Batman meets Aquaman with a side of Bruce Wayne.

1. Using a brush or a clean steel wool pad, scrub the grit from each of the oyster shells and rinse them under cold, running water. Grasp an oyster in one hand, cup-side down, insert an oyster knife into the opening, and run it from top to bottom of the hinge, which should open it. If the hinge doesn't open, try giving the knife a small twist in the center of the hinge. Using your fingers, remove the top shell of each oyster. Be sure to save their juice (liquor) in a small bowl. Set the juices aside at room temperature. Gently clean off any dark parts around the oyster meat. Keep the oysters in their bottom shell, and set aside in the fridge. 2. In a medium-size saucepan, combine the cream and cheese over medium heat. Once the cheese is starting to melt, add the reserved oyster juice and port wine. Turn down the heat to low and cook, stirring, for 8 to 10 minutes, or until the liquid has reduced by half. Season to taste with salt and pepper. 3. Just before serving, fill a shallow saucepan with a steamer insert with 3 cups (750 mL) of water over medium-high heat to steam the oysters. Once the water is boiling, place the oysters, shell side down, on the steam rack, and steam, covered, for about 1 minute. Remove the pan from the heat and carefully remove the oysters. 4. Slide an oyster knife between the oyster meat and the shell to loosen the lower adductors, keeping the meat in the bottom shell. Place the oysters on a serving plate and pour equal amounts of cheesy liquid on each. Sprinkle with finely chopped walnuts and serve immediately.

Party!

SERVES 7–10

Mango Chutney

2 cups (500 mL) ripe mango, finely diced

½ cup (125 mL) diced red bell pepper

½ cup (125 mL) diced shallots

½ cup (125 mL) raisins

¼ cup (60 mL) brown sugar, packed

1 Tbsp (15 mL) ground turmeric

1 Tbsp (15 mL) ground ginger

1 tsp (5 mL) ground allspice

3 Tbsp (45 mL) red wine vinegar

Kosher salt and freshly ground black pepper

Samosas

1 1-lb (450 g) package store-bought, all-butter
   puff pastry

16 medium oysters

4 cloves garlic

1 large white onion, roughly chopped

¼ cup (60 mL) mint leaves

1 Tbsp (15 mL) yellow curry powder

1 Tbsp (15 mL) ground coriander

1 Tbsp (15 mL) garam marsala

2 Tbsp (30 mL) olive oil

2 cups (500 mL) canola oil

OYSTER SAMOSAS

Did someone say "samosa"? These crispy, savory, and fragrant snacks are so good for party platters. They're easy to prep beforehand, so you can spend time with your guests and not feel as though you're stuck in the kitchen for all the best parts of the night.

1. Thaw out the puff pastry overnight in the refrigerator before using, but keep it refrigerated until you're ready to use it. 2. To make the mango chutney, place the mango, bell peppers, shallots, raisins, sugar, turmeric, ginger, allspice, and vinegar in a large saucepan over medium heat. Cook, stirring occasionally, for 30 to 45 minutes, or until the ingredients are soft. Season to taste with salt and pepper, remove from the heat, and set aside. If you prefer to serve this dish with cold mango chutney, you can transfer the chutney to a bowl and place it in the refrigerator, covered, to cool for 30 to 45 minutes before serving. The chutney will keep in the fridge for 2 weeks. 3. Using a brush or a clean steel wool pad, scrub the grit from each of the oyster shells and rinse them under cold, running water. Grasp an oyster in one hand, cup-side down, insert an oyster knife into the opening, and run it from top to bottom of the hinge, which should open it. If the hinge doesn't open, try giving the knife a small twist in the center of the hinge. Using your fingers, remove the top shell of each oyster. Slip the oyster knife under the oyster meat to loosen the lower adductors, allowing you to remove the meat and discard the liquor. Gently clean off any dark parts around the oyster meat. Finely chop the meat and set it aside in the fridge until needed. Discard the shells. 4. In a food processor fitted with the steel blade, place the garlic, onions, mint, curry powder, coriander, and garam marsala. Process until finely diced and well mixed. 5. In a large sauté pan over medium heat, heat the olive oil. Combine the

oyster meat and onion mixture. Stir well and then cook for 10 to 12 minutes, or until cooked through, stirring occasionally. Remove from the heat and allow to cool at room temperature. 6. On a clean work surface, roll out the puff pastry, if it isn't pre-rolled already. Cut it into 2- x 2-inch (5 x 5 cm) squares. Be sure to work quickly, because if it dries out or melts, you're going to be in trouble. 7. Place 1 tsp (5 mL) of oyster filling in the center of each pastry piece, and fold one half over to create a triangle pocket. Brush the edges of the pastry with a little water and then use your fingers or the tines of a fork to seal the pastry tight. If you have extra filling, it's a great addition to scrambled eggs. 8. If you'd like to serve the chutney warm, place it back on the stove top over low heat, stirring occasionally, for 5 to 7 minutes, or until heated through. 9. In a medium-size saucepan, heat the canola oil to 350°F (180°C). Use a cooking thermometer to check the temperature. Line a plate with paper towels. 10. Working in small batches and using a metal slotted spoon, carefully place the pastries, a few at a time to avoid overcrowding the pan, into the hot oil, and fry for 1 to 2 minutes, turning once, or until golden brown and puffy. Using the slotted spoon again, remove them from the oil and place them on the prepared plate to absorb any excess oil. Allow the oil to come back up to temperature before proceeding with the next batch. 11. Serve samosas with the mango chutney.

NOTE: *You can make these samosas a couple of days ahead of time. Allow them to cool, and then place them in the freezer, wrapped in aluminum foil, to store—they'll keep for about 3 months. When you're ready to eat them, remove the samosas from the freezer and bake from frozen at 375°F (190°C), on a baking tray, for 12 to 15 minutes, or until they're heated all the way through.*

SERVES 6

Fig Jam

1 lb (450 g) fresh figs, roughly chopped

2 cups (500 mL) granulated sugar

Juice and zest from 1 orange

Oysters

12 oysters

1 tsp (5 mL) brown sugar

1 Tbsp (15 mL) lemon juice

6 long slices pancetta, cut in half widthwise

PANCETTA-WRAPPED OYSTERS & FIG JAM

This recipe was inspired by my mother, who loves to wrap anything and everything in bacon. She wraps bacon around cubes of white bread and then smothers them in mushroom soup and bakes them. I know it sounds odd, but I have to admit that it's my favorite treat that my mom makes for my sister, Amie, and me. I choose to use "fancy" bacon (pancetta) to take this recipe to the next level. It's cool if you don't like fig jam—just use any other jam that floats your boat! And remember that this recipe can easily be doubled for larger gatherings too.

1. To make the fig jam, place the figs, sugar, and orange juice and zest in a saucepan over low heat. Stir to dissolve the sugar. Increase the heat to medium-high and bring to a boil, stirring regularly. Once boiling, turn down the heat to medium and cook, stirring occasionally, for approximately 45 minutes, or until thick and sticky. Transfer to mason jars with tight-fitting lids, and store the jam in the refrigerator for up to 1 month. 2. Preheat the oven to 350°F (180°C). Line a baking tray with aluminum foil. 3. Using a brush or a clean steel wool pad, scrub the grit from each of the oyster shells and rinse them under cold, running water. Grasp an oyster in one hand, cup-side down, and insert an oyster knife into the opening and run it from top to bottom of the hinge, which should open it. If the hinge doesn't open, try giving the knife a small twist in the center of the hinge. Using your fingers, remove the top shell of each oyster. Gently clean off any dark parts around the oyster meat. Slip the oyster knife under the oyster meat to loosen the lower adductors, allowing you to remove the meat and discard the liquor. Keep the oyster meat intact, and discard the shells. 4. In a small bowl, combine the brown sugar and lemon juice. Using a pastry brush, brush each pancetta piece on both sides with some of the sugar mixture. Roll the pancetta strips around each oyster meat, covering the entire piece of meat. Place them on the prepared baking tray and bake for 10 to 12 minutes, flipping once, or until the pancetta is crispy. 5. Serve the oysters hot with the fig jam for dipping.

Brunch

PICKLED RAW OYSTERS

SERVES 4

12 medium oysters

2 cloves garlic, crushed

½ cup (125 mL) thinly sliced
   white onion

½ cup (125 mL) white wine
   vinegar

¼ cup (60 mL) lemon juice
   (about 2 lemons)

2 tsp (10 mL) granulated sugar

½ tsp (2 mL) chili flakes

½ tsp (2 mL) kosher salt

8–12 whole cracked black
   peppercorns

4 sesame seed bagels,
   toasted, or 4 slices crispy
   sourdough bread, to serve

Cream cheese or your favorite
   spread, to serve

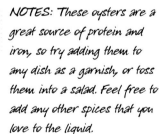

NOTES: These oysters are a
great source of protein and
iron, so try adding them to
any dish as a garnish, or toss
them into a salad. Feel free to
add any other spices that you
love to the liquid.

This super-simple, quick pickling recipe is foolproof. Pickling is all the rage in restaurants, and it's easy to understand why: not only are pickled foods delicious, but pickling is a great way to extend food's shelf life. Most people don't pickle seafood as often as they pickle vegetables, eggs, or ham, but this is a shellfish cookbook, so let's have some fun!

1. Using a brush or a clean steel wool pad, scrub the grit from each of the oyster shells and rinse them under cold, running water. Grasp an oyster in one hand, cup-side down, insert an oyster knife into the opening, and run it from top to bottom of the hinge, which should open it. If the hinge doesn't open, try giving the knife a small twist in the center of the hinge. Using your fingers, remove the top shell of each oyster. Gently clean off any dark parts around the oyster meat. Slip the oyster knife under the oyster meat to loosen the lower adductors, allowing you to remove the meat. Keeping the meat intact, place it in a bowl. Place ¼ cup (60 mL) of the oyster's liquor in a medium-size saucepan. Discard the shells. 2. Add the garlic, onions, vinegar, lemon juice, sugar, chili flakes, salt, and peppercorns to the oyster liquor. This will be your pickling liquid. Bring to a boil, then reduce to a simmer for approximately 5 minutes over medium-high heat. 3. Transfer the pickling liquid to a bowl and place it in the refrigerator, covered, to cool and to allow the flavors to combine. 4. Once the pickling liquid is cool, pour it over the oysters, making sure the oysters are completely submerged. Cover the bowl in plastic wrap and place in the refrigerator for a minimum of 2 hours to allow the oysters to pickle. 5. Keep the pickled oysters for up to 1 week in an airtight container in the refrigerator. Try them on top of a toasted bagel with cream cheese, or on a crispy slice of sourdough bread with your favorite spread.

Lunch

SERVES 2

8 oysters

1 Tbsp (15 mL) canola oil

1 Tbsp (15 mL) Cajun seasoning, divided

¼ cup (60 mL) full-fat mayonnaise

Kosher salt and freshly ground black pepper

2 ciabatta buns, sliced in half lengthwise

¼ head iceberg lettuce, shredded

6 slices on-the-vine tomatoes

4 medium pickles, cut into thin coins

Lemon Caper Dip (page 225) or Sriracha Mayo (page 226), for drizzling

NOTE: Rumor has it that the po-boy was invented in the late 1800s. Make sure to check out Acme Oyster House when in N'awlins, for the best po-boy, in my humble opinion!

SPICY NEW ORLEANS OYSTER PO-BOY

New Orleans is one of the best cities in the USA, especially if you're a music lover like I am. A N'awlins night often goes like this: grab a big meal, wash it down with some bourbon or craft beers, and then pop into a bunch of live music bars, all playing different jams along Frenchmen Street. Cap the evening off with oyster po-boys, and call it a night.

1. Using a brush or a clean steel wool pad, scrub the grit from each of the oyster shells and rinse them under cold, running water. Grasp an oyster in one hand, cup-side down, insert an oyster knife into the opening, and run it from top to bottom of the hinge, which should open it. If the hinge doesn't open, try giving the knife a small twist in the center of the hinge. Using your fingers, remove the top shell of each oyster. Gently clean off any dark parts around the oyster meat. Slip the oyster knife under the oyster meat to loosen the lower adductors, allowing you to remove the meat and discard the liquor. Keep the meat intact. Discard the shells. 2. Toss the oyster meat in a bowl with the canola oil and 1 ½ tsp (7 mL) of the Cajun seasoning to coat them. 3. In a medium-size skillet over medium-high heat, sauté the oysters for 2 to 3 minutes per side, until crispy and golden brown, and then remove them from the heat. 4. In a mixing bowl, mix together the mayonnaise and the remaining 1 ½ tsp (7 mL) of Cajun seasoning. Season to taste with salt and pepper. 5. Spread the Cajun mayo onto the bottom half of each bun. Top with lettuce, tomatoes, and pickle slices. Place the crispy cooked oysters on top, and drizzle with Lemon Caper Dip or Sriracha Mayo. Close the sandwich and eat immediately.

Celeb Chef

SERVES 6–8

1 lb (450 g) haddock

12 oysters

1 lb (450 g) live mussels, cleaned and debearded

1 lb (450 g) littleneck clams

1 cup (250 mL) diced Yukon Gold potatoes

4 cups (1 L) whole (3.5%) milk

½ cup (125 mL) dried Irish moss (whole, if possible; see note)

Cold, unsalted butter, for garnish (optional)

2 Tbsp (30 mL) dulse powder (optional)

Kosher salt and freshly ground black pepper (optional)

1 loaf of fresh sourdough bread

Special equipment

Smoker

Irish turf or maple wood chips

THATCHED COTTAGE CHOWDER
BY PATRICK MCMURRAY A.K.A. SHUCKER PADDY

In 2015, I was competing in the Ocean Wise Chowder Challenge and I was seeking inspiration for which dish to make. I used the movie *The Secret of Roan Inish* as my inspiration that year. I thought about an Irish chowder, something that would have been cooked 100 years ago in a whitewashed stone cottage with a thatched roof in Donegal, in Northern Ireland. The film has a scene where a selkie (a mermaid) creates a restorative soup from seaweed. I figured that back then, all food was made in an open hearth, fired by turf, which is peat moss bricks of compressed vegetation that gives off the distinctive smell of remote Irish thatched-roof cottages. I knew this award-winning recipe (yes, it won!) would be the perfect dish for MDP's shellfish cookbook.

1. First, smoke the haddock for about 10 minutes, according to your smoker's instructions, using Irish turf or maple wood chips. You're looking to add flavor, not to thoroughly cook the fish—that will happen in the chowder-making process.
2. Next, open the oysters. Using a brush or a clean steel wool pad, scrub the grit from each of the oyster shells and rinse them under cold, running water. Grasp an oyster in one hand, cup-side down, insert an oyster knife into the opening, and run it from top to bottom of the hinge, which should open it. If the hinge doesn't open, try giving the knife a small twist in the center of the hinge. Using your fingers, remove the top shell of each oyster. Gently clean off any dark parts around the oyster meat. Slip the oyster knife under the oyster meat to loosen the lower adductors, allowing you to remove the meat and discard the liquor. Discard the shells, but make sure to keep the liquor. 3. Add the liquor to a large saucepan over medium heat. Add the cleaned mussels, cover the pan with a tight-fitting lid, and allow them to steam open in the liquor for about 4 minutes. (If you want to remove the mussel shells before you serve the soup, then this is the best time to do so. Take the saucepan off the heat, remove the shells, keeping the meat intact, and place the meat back in the saucepan. Put the saucepan back on medium heat.) 4. Add the oyster meats, the clams still in their shells, the potatoes, and the milk, and turn down the heat to medium-low so as not to scald or split the soup. Once warm, add the smoked haddock, in large pieces, as it will flake apart once cooked. Add the Irish moss—it will expand and soften, and the soup will thicken. Once the soup has steam

coming off its surface and is hot to taste, the moss will be soft and textural, the soup will be velvety, and the fish will be cooked through. 5. When you serve this soup, make sure everyone gets their fair share of the shellfish. If you wish, add a dollop of cold butter on the top and dulse powder to season. Dulse powder is a finely ground seaweed and is my version of salt. If you choose not to use the dulse powder, check your seasonings and add salt and pepper to taste. Serve with a thick slice of sourdough bread to clean the bowl.

NOTE: You can find Irish moss in health food stores or at your local fishmonger's. Or give me a shout on Twitter (@ShuckerPaddy) and I'll tell my friends in Skinners Pond, Prince Edward Island, to save some for you!

SCALLO

SERVES 2–4

1 lb (450 g) large sea
 scallops (U10 size/count)

Kosher salt and freshly ground
 black pepper

1 Tbsp (15 mL) canola oil

1 Tbsp (15 mL) unsalted butter

Fresh thyme leaves, for garnish

PERFECT PAN-SEARED SCALLOPS

This recipe will teach you the basic, fundamental skills for cooking perfect scallops. The key to perfect pan-seared scallops is actually quite simple: you want to use a very hot, nonstick pan with a combo of butter and oil, and you do not want to move the scallops while they're searing. As you know, practice makes perfect, so have fun perfecting your scallop game!

1. To sear scallops perfectly, they must be bone-dry. Before you cook the scallops, take them out of the refrigerator, let them sit at room temperature for 10 to 15 minutes, and then pat them dry with paper towels. 2. Season the scallops with salt and pepper on both sides. 3. Using a good-quality nonstick pan, heat the canola oil and butter over high heat. Keep a close eye on the pan to ensure that it's very hot, but not smoking, before you add the scallops. 4. Using tongs, carefully place the scallops in the pan. Do not move them. If the pan is too hot and begins to smoke, simply lower the heat ever so slightly. 5. Sear each scallop on the first side for approximately 2 minutes, or until you see a nice golden brown crust. Using tongs again, carefully turn the scallops over and sear the opposite side for 45 seconds to 1 minute. The scallops should be soft to the touch, golden brown on the outside, and translucent in the middle. 6. Allow the scallops to rest for 1 to 2 minutes before serving them with their best seared side up. Garnish with fresh thyme leaves. This dish works especially well over a beautiful rice or pasta dish.

Party!

SERVES 9–10

½ cup (125 mL) green beans, cut into ¼-inch (6 mm) pieces

3 Tbsp (45 mL) extra-virgin olive oil, divided

2 cloves garlic, finely chopped

1 large shallot, finely diced

¼ cup (60 mL) dry white wine

1 can (19 oz/540 mL) cannellini beans, drained and rinsed

6 slices thick-cut strip bacon, cooked and cut into ¼-inch (6 mm) cubes

Kosher salt and freshly ground black pepper

18 diver scallops (U10 size/ count)

¼ cup (60 mL) microgreens, for garnish

BACON SEA SCALLOP SPOONS

I love the ingredients in this recipe because they remind me of my travels to Italy, where cannellini beans and white wine are commonly used—and make for a killer combo. Of course, feel free to plate this in any way you see fit, but I think these one-bite spoons are simply perfect.

1. First, blanch the green beans. Bring a small saucepan with 3 cups (750 mL) of cold water to a boil over high heat. While this water comes to a boil, prepare a bowl with 3 cups (750 mL) of very cold water and ice cubes. Carefully place the green beans in the boiling water and blanch for 30 seconds to 1 minute, or until the beans turn bright green. Using a slotted spoon, remove the beans from the boiling water and place them in the ice water right away. 2. In a medium-size sauté pan, heat 1 Tbsp (15 mL) of the olive oil over medium-high heat. Add the garlic and shallots. Sauté for 2 to 3 minutes, or until soft and fragrant. Add the wine and stir to deglaze the pan. Add the green beans, cannellini beans, and bacon. Stir well and then let the mixture sit over the heat to bring all the ingredients up to a boil. Cook for 3 to 5 minutes, or until most of the liquid boils off, season to taste with salt and pepper, and remove from the heat. Keep warm. 3. Meanwhile, in a large sauté pan, heat the remaining 2 Tbsp (30 mL) of olive oil over medium-high heat. Working in small batches, use tongs to place the scallops in the hot oil and sear for 1 ½ to 2 minutes, without touching them. Using tongs again, turn each scallop over and sear the other side. This time only cook them for 45 to 60 seconds. Remove them from the pan, place them on a plate, and let them rest for 1 to 2 minutes before serving. 4. Set out 18 serving spoons on a large plate or board (tablespoons will work if you don't have fancy spoons). Carefully spoon a small amount of hot bean mixture onto the bottom of each spoon. Place a warm scallop on top of the bean mixture and garnish with microgreens. Any leftover bean mixture can be used in a salad or as a side dish.

Brunch

SERVES 4–6

8 small red potatoes

1 Tbsp (15 mL) unsalted butter

1 lb (450 g) small bay
   scallops (80/120 size/
   count)

4 green onions, coarsely
   chopped

½ cup (125 mL) fresh summer
   savory (see note)

¼ cup (60 mL) full-fat
   mayonnaise

Juice from 1 lemon

Kosher salt and freshly ground
   black pepper

1 tsp (5 mL) smoked paprika

¼ cup (60 mL) microgreens,
   for garnish

6 slices of good-quality bread,
   cut into thick slices (optional)

NOTE: Buy savory as fresh
as possible, but if you can't
find it fresh, use fresh sage
or thyme, which have similar
tasting notes.

BAY SCALLOP POTATO SALAD

This recipe calls for a well-known Canadian herb called summer savory, which you'll find at its freshest on the East Coast. Savory has a peppery taste, adds a great flavor to any dish, and is one of the herbs in the French seasoning herbes de Provence.

1. Fill a large saucepan with 4 cups (1 L) of cold water. Add the whole potatoes and bring to a boil. Boil the potatoes for 12 to 15 minutes, or until a fork pierces them easily. Remove from the heat, drain, and allow to cool at room temperature. Take care not to overcook the potatoes, as you want them in solid pieces and not falling apart. Once the potatoes are cool, slice them in half. 2. Meanwhile, to prepare the scallops, melt the butter in a large sauté pan over medium-high heat. Place the scallops in the pan and cook, stirring occasionally, for 3 to 4 minutes, or until slightly brown. Do not overcook them. Set aside at room temperature until cool enough to handle. 3. In a large mixing bowl, place the cooked potato halves, cooked scallops, green onions, summer savory, mayonnaise, and lemon juice. Season to taste with salt and pepper. Gently stir to combine. Cover the bowl and place it in the refrigerator for at least 30 minutes to cool. 4. Sprinkle the cold salad with the paprika and microgreens just before serving. I love this potato salad piled high on fresh, thick-cut slices of bread, but you can also serve it as a side dish.

Party!

DIVER SCALLOP ROCKEFELLER

SERVES 4

8 diver scallops, shell on

2 cups (500 mL) spinach, stems discarded

¾ cup (175 mL) dry white wine

1 small white onion, finely chopped

2 Tbsp (30 mL) unsalted butter

1 bay leaf

1 tsp (5 mL) cayenne pepper

1 tsp (5 mL) ground nutmeg

1 tsp (5 mL) Dijon mustard

¼ cup (60 mL) 2% milk

½ cup (125 mL) Kosher or rock salt

½ cup (125 mL) grated Provolone cheese

½ cup (125 mL) Panko breadcrumbs

I used to serve this dish in my restaurants for special occasions like Valentine's Day. It was always a fan favorite as the scallops, which are already packed full of sea brine flavor, are taken to the next level thanks to all the other rich ingredients. Diver scallops are not readily available all year, so check in at your local specialty fish store to see when they'll be in season. They're worth the wait, because they're sweet, sustainable, and delicious. This recipe can easily be doubled for larger gatherings.

1. Preheat the oven to 375°F (190°C). 2. Hold a scallop with the dark side of the shell facing up. Carefully place an oyster knife between the shells, in the hinge, and give a slight twist to pop it open. Discard the top shell. Gently clean the scallop under cold, running water and remove all the orange-red innards, leaving only the scallop attached to the shell. Repeat with the remaining scallops. Set aside in the fridge until needed. 3. To blanch the spinach, in a medium-size saucepan, bring 3 cups (750 mL) of cold water to a boil over high heat. While this water comes to a boil, prepare a small bowl with ¾ cup (175 mL) of cold water and a few ice cubes. Carefully place the spinach leaves in the boiling water, and blanch for 30 seconds to 1 minute, or until the spinach turns bright green. Using a slotted spoon, remove the blanched spinach from the boiling water and place it into the ice water right away. Using your hand, lift out the spinach and squeeze any excess water from it. Transfer the spinach to a sieve and set it aside at room temperature to continue to drain. 4. In a medium-size sauté pan over medium-high heat, place the wine, onions, butter, and bay leaf. Cook for 3 to 4 minutes, or until the onions are soft, translucent, and fragrant and most of the wine has evaporated. Add the cayenne pepper, mix well, and then remove the pan from the heat but keep the burner on. 5. Drain off any excess liquid from the mixture and bring the pan back to the burner. Add the blanched spinach, nutmeg, and mustard. Mix well, add the milk, and stir again. Turn down the heat to low and simmer for 2 to 3 minutes, or until all the milk has been absorbed into the mixture. 6. Line a baking tray with enough kosher or rock salt to keep the scallops in place. 7. Lay the scallops, still in their shell, on the prepared baking tray. 8. Spoon 1 Tbsp (15 mL) of the hot mixture into each of the shells, and top with a healthy pinch of cheese and breadcrumbs. Bake the scallops for 5 to 7 minutes, or until the cheese is golden brown and bubbling. 9. Serve hot with a great glass of crisp white wine.

Dinner

FALL HARVEST SCALLOPS

SERVES 2–4

1 small head cauliflower, stem removed

Extra-virgin olive oil, for drizzling

Kosher salt and freshly ground black pepper

1 cup (250 mL) 2% milk

1 Tbsp (15 mL) unsalted butter

1 tsp (5 mL) ground nutmeg

½ cup (125 mL) black beluga or Puy lentils, picked over and rinsed

1 Tbsp (15 mL) canola oil

1 lb (450 g) sea scallops (U10 size/count)

2 small heirloom carrots, washed and sliced into long, thin ribbons with a vegetable peeler

¼ cup (60 mL) baby arugula

¼ cup (60 mL) toasted pumpkin seeds

1 Tbsp (15 mL) honey

I grew up in Midland, Ontario, which is about two hours north of Toronto. The fall scenery always makes me think of home. Every year my family gets together for a huge Thanksgiving baseball game, followed by a great meal. I love seeing the vibrant fall colors of the leaves and enjoying the amazing fall fruit and vegetables. And it's great to see my family, of course! I absolutely love these kinds of moments!

1. Preheat the oven to 375°F (190°C). **2.** Place the head of cauliflower on a baking tray, drizzle it with extra-virgin olive oil, and season to taste with salt and pepper. Roast in the oven for 20 to 25 minutes, or until soft enough to pierce easily with a knife. Remove the cauliflower from the oven, let it cool enough to handle, and then chop it into small florets. Using a food processor fitted with the steel blade, blend the cauliflower until smooth. **3.** In a medium-size saucepan over medium-high heat, place the cauliflower purée and milk. Bring to a simmer and cook, stirring occasionally, for 8 to 10 minutes, or until the milk has been completely absorbed. Add the butter, nutmeg, and salt and pepper to taste. Using a hand blender or potato masher, pulse it into a smooth purée. Keep it warm until needed, but be careful not to burn it. **4.** Meanwhile, in a medium-size saucepan, bring 1 ½ cups (375 mL) of cold water to a boil over medium-high heat. Add the lentils and then immediately turn down the heat to medium. Cover the saucepan and simmer for 15 to 18 minutes, or until the lentils are tender. Drain the lentils and return them to the saucepan to keep warm until needed. **5.** In a medium-size sauté pan, heat the canola oil over high heat, until hot but not smoking. **6.** Using tongs, carefully place the scallops in the pan. Sear them for 2 to 3 minutes, without touching them at all. Once a brown crust has formed and the scallops release easily from the pan, use the tongs to gently turn them over and cook the other side for 45 seconds to 1 minute. You may need to do this step in batches. **7.** Smear some cauliflower purée on serving plates and top with three to four scallops each. Top each scallop with a healthy spoonful of lentils, followed by a few carrot ribbons. Evenly distribute the arugula and pumpkin seeds among the dishes and drizzle with honey to finish.

FRIED COCONUT SEA SCALLOPS

SERVES 2–4

1 lb (450 g) sea scallops (U10 size/count)

2 cloves garlic, minced

Juice from 1 lemon

1 cup (250 mL) chickpea flour

3 large eggs, beaten

2 cups (500 mL) Panko breadcrumbs

1 cup (250 mL) shredded unsweetened coconut

2 cups (500 mL) canola oil

¼ cup (60 mL) Sriracha Mayo (page 226)

When I was a child, my parents used to order coconut shrimp for me all the time. I would eat them and be as happy as a clam—fitting for this book, though I've swapped shrimp for scallops. One of the first times I remember eating coconut shrimp was when I was about 8 years old. We were at an old Toronto landmark restaurant called the Bamboo Club, on Queen Street West. It's since closed down, but that place rocked and my parents loved taking me there. Maybe that's why I love seafood so much!

1. In a large bowl, place the scallops, garlic, and lemon juice. Gently mix to coat the scallops thoroughly and evenly. Cover and refrigerate for 25 to 30 minutes to marinate. 2. Remove the scallops from the refrigerator and allow to come to room temperature. 3. Set up a dredging station by placing the flour in a small bowl and the beaten eggs in another small bowl, and combining the breadcrumbs and coconut in a medium-size bowl. 4. In a medium-size saucepan, heat the canola oil over medium-high heat to 350°F (180°C). Use a cooking thermometer to check the temperature. Line a plate with paper towels. 5. Dredge the scallops in the flour, then the eggs, and then in the breadcrumb mixture. Coat evenly. Lay the dredged scallops on a plate until you're ready to fry them. 6. Working in small batches so you don't overcrowd the pan, use tongs to place the coated scallops in the hot oil. Fry for 1 to 2 minutes, turning once, or until golden brown and crispy. The scallops should float to the top of the oil when they are ready. Transfer them to the prepared plate to absorb any excess oil. 7. Transfer the scallops to a serving platter and serve while still hot, with my Sriracha Mayo for dipping.

Dinner

ROASTED SCALLOPS WITH CIDER & CREAM

SERVES 2–4

⅓ cup (75 mL) dry cider

⅓ cup + 2 Tbsp (105 mL) extra-virgin olive oil

¼ cup (60 mL) heavy (35%) cream

Juice from 1 ½ lemons, divided

3 Tbsp (45 mL) unsalted butter

2 cloves garlic, minced

3 Tbsp (45 mL) finely chopped curly parsley

Kosher salt and freshly ground black pepper

1 medium green apple

1 lb (450 g) sea scallops (U10 size/count)

Cider isn't just for drinking—you can cook with it too. I find that it adds a fresh, acidic note to any dish. In this recipe, it also helps to balance the richness of the cream. I like Brickworks Cider for this as it's crisp and dry and adds just a hint of sweetness.

1. Preheat the oven to 375°F (190°C). 2. In a large sauté pan over medium heat, place the cider, ⅓ cup (75 mL) of the olive oil, the cream, juice from 1 lemon, and the butter, followed by the garlic and parsley. Mix well and sauté for 8 to 10 minutes, stirring occasionally, until the sauce starts to thicken. Season to taste with salt and pepper. Turn down the heat to a simmer while you cook the scallops. 3. While the sauce reduces, peel and cut the apple into matchstick pieces and place them in a bowl, tossed in the remaining lemon juice to stop them from browning. 4. In a separate large sauté pan, place the remaining 2 Tbsp (30 mL) of olive oil and heat it over medium-high heat. 5. Using tongs, carefully place the scallops in the pan. Sear the scallops for 2 to 3 minutes, without touching them at all. Once a brown crust has formed and the scallops releases easily from the pan, use the tongs to gently turn them over and cook the other side for 45 seconds to 1 minute. You may have to do this in batches. 6. Transfer the scallops to serving plates and spoon the cider cream sauce evenly over each one. Any leftover sauce can be stored in the fridge for 3 to 4 days. Garnish with the apple pieces.

SPANISH SCALLOPS WITH CRUSTY BREAD

SERVES 4

6 cloves garlic

¼ cup (60 mL) extra-virgin olive oil, plus extra for drizzling

2 cups (500 mL) crushed tomatoes

2 lb (900 g) bay scallops (80/120 size/count)

1 Tbsp (15 mL) sweet paprika

Kosher salt and freshly ground black pepper

¼ cup (60 mL) dry white wine

¼ cup (60 mL) dry sherry

½ loaf crusty bread

¼ cup (60 mL) finely chopped flat-leaf parsley

Some of Europe's best dishes are the simplest ones, it seems, and they always start with the best of the best ingredients. Picture making this dish in a small seaside village in Spain with fresh tomatoes, a variety of spices, hand-selected olive oil, and delicious crusty bread. If you don't happen to be in Spain as you're cooking this, just select the freshest, juiciest produce and ingredients you have access to and let your imagination do the rest of the work.

1. Preheat the oven to 425°F (220°C). 2. Mince four of the garlic cloves. 3. In a large sauté pan over medium-high heat, sauté the minced garlic in the olive oil for 1 to 2 minutes, or until the garlic is fragrant. Add the crushed tomatoes and mix well. Turn the heat to medium and cook for 3 to 4 minutes, stirring occasionally. 4. Add the scallops, paprika, and salt and pepper to taste. Continue to cook for 1 to 2 minutes, or until the scallops are soft and opaque. Slowly add the wine and dry sherry to the pan and stir well. Cook for 2 to 3 minutes to allow the flavors to combine and then remove the pan from the heat. Be very careful not to overcook the bay scallops, as they can become rubbery quite quickly. 5. Slice each of the two remaining garlic cloves in half lengthwise. 6. Cut the crusty bread into slices, about ½-inch (1.2 cm) thick. Drizzle each slice with extra-virgin olive oil and, using the exposed end of the raw garlic cloves, rub the garlic overtop. Place the bread slices on a baking tray, oil side up, and toast for 6 to 8 minutes, flipping once, or until toasted and golden brown in color. 7. Spoon the tomato–scallop mixture into serving bowls and garnish with the flat-leaf parsley. Enjoy the toasted bread dipped into the sauce!

Lunch

SERVES 6–8

½ cup (125 mL) olive oil

4 limes, juiced and divided

1 Tbsp (15 mL) chili powder

6 cloves garlic, finely diced

½ cup (125 mL) chopped
   cilantro leaves

1 Tbsp (15 mL) ground cumin

1 Tbsp (15 mL) dried oregano

2 lb (900 g) sea scallops
   (U10 size/count)

4 ears of corn, cut into 2- to
   3-inch (5–8 cm) pieces

2 medium red bell peppers,
   seeded and cut into 2-inch
   (5 cm) chunks

1 large red onion, cut into
   2-inch (5 cm) chunks

½ cup (125 mL) full-fat sour
   cream

1 tsp (5 mL) chili flakes

Kosher salt and freshly ground
   black pepper

Special equipment

Metal skewers

TIJUANA MEXICO SCALLOP SKEWERS

Funnily enough, this recipe is inspired by my travels to San Diego, California, and not Mexico! While in San Diego, I kept seeing Tijuana skewers dressed with lots of ingredients on various menus. These make for a perfect appetizer for any lunch gathering or backyard party. If you want to add another nice touch on this dish, crumble Cotija cheese to garnish the finished skewers. Cotija cheese is from Mexico. It has a similar texture to feta but it's less salty.

1. In a large airtight container, place the olive oil, juice from three of the limes, chili powder, garlic, cilantro, cumin, and oregano. Stir to combine and then add the scallops, corn, bell peppers, and onions. Mix thoroughly so that all the ingredients are well coated in the marinade. Place the lid on the container and put it in the refrigerator for 3 to 6 hours. 2. Preheat the barbecue to 375°F (190°C). Season the grill with nonstick cooking spray or canola oil. 3. In a small mixing bowl, combine the remaining lime juice, the sour cream, and chili flakes. Transfer the mixture to a squeeze bottle or resealable plastic bag and place it in the refrigerator until needed. 4. To assemble the skewers, place a piece of marinated corn, then bell pepper, scallop, onion, and then another piece of corn to close the skewer. Repeat until all the skewers are complete and season with salt and pepper to taste. 5. Cook each of the skewers on the grill, carefully rotating halfway through, for 5 to 7 minutes, or until the scallops are soft and translucent. Drizzle the sour cream sauce on top of the skewers and serve immediately.

Quick & Easy

SERVES 2–4

1 lb (450 g) bay scallops (80/120 size/count), diced small

¼ cup (60 mL) finely diced English cucumber, skin on

1 small jalapeño pepper, seeded and finely diced

1 large avocado, finely diced

2 Tbsp (30 mL) black and white sesame seeds, combined, plus extra for garnish

1 Tbsp (15 mL) sesame oil

2 limes, quartered and divided

1 cup (250 mL) canola oil

1 1-lb (450 g) package wonton wrappers

Kosher salt

4 small radishes, finely sliced

SCALLOP TARTARE

Tartare of any sort is my jam! I love it because you can make it with almost any protein that can be chopped and served raw. The fresh, clean flavors of the ingredients I use here make this dish simply irresistible. Feel free to substitute albacore tuna, shrimp, lobster, or any other fresh fish in place of the scallops.

1. In a large mixing bowl, place the diced scallops, cucumbers, jalapeño, avocados, sesame seeds, and sesame oil. Squeeze the juice from two of the lime quarters overtop. Gently mix, cover, and refrigerate for a minimum of 1 hour to allow the flavors to combine. 2. In a medium-size saucepan, bring the canola oil to 350°F (180°C) over medium-high heat. Use a cooking thermometer to check the temperature. Line a plate with paper towels. 3. Working in small batches to avoid overcrowding the pan, use tongs to carefully lower the wonton wrappers into the oil. Fry for 1 to 2 minutes, or until the wontons are crisp and light golden. Using tongs again, remove the wontons from the oil and place them on the prepared plate to cool and absorb any excess oil. Season with salt to taste. 4. In the middle of a circular serving plate, fan out the thin slices of radishes in an attractive manner. Carefully spoon the scallop tartare mixture into the middle of the plate, letting the radishes show through. Garnish with extra sesame seeds, wonton chips, and the remaining six lime quarters. Serve immediately.

SHRIMP & PRAWNS

Lunch

BUFFALO SHRIMP & CAULIFLOWER POUTINE

SERVES 4

1 ½ cups (375 mL) canola oil

1 cup (250 mL) all-purpose flour, plus more for dusting

4 medium eggs

1 head cauliflower, stem removed, chopped into small florets

1 lb (450 g) large U.S. wild shrimp, peeled and deveined

Kosher salt

1 cup (250 mL) fresh or canned, drained corn kernels

½ cup (125 mL) bruschetta mix (see note)

¼ cup (60 mL) green onions, sliced lengthwise

½ cup (125 mL) crumbled blue cheese

½ cup (125 mL) Sriracha Mayo (page 226)

NOTE: To make your own bruschetta mix, dice half of a large, ripe tomato and a quarter of a white onion. Finely mince a garlic clove, then combine all ingredients. Keep refrigerated until needed.

With this recipe I've added a fun, new twist to a Canadian staple: poutine, which ought to be recognized as our national dish. I'm using cauliflower instead of french fries—the cool thing about this dish is that you can change and add as many toppings as you like. I like to use U.S. wild shrimp for this as they're sustainably sourced. If you're looking for a classic poutine, try my famous lobster poutine from my first book, *The Great Lobster Cookbook*!

1. In a medium-size saucepan, bring the canola oil to 350°F (180°C) over medium-high heat. 2. Set up a dredging station by placing the flour in a small bowl and whisking the eggs in a second bowl. 3. Dredge each cauliflower floret and shrimp in the bowl of flour, then the egg mixture, and then the flour again. Shake off any excess flour. 4. Line a plate with paper towels. 5. Working in small batches so you don't overcrowd the pan, use tongs to carefully place the cauliflower florets in the hot oil, continually turning them over, frying for 2 to 3 minutes, or until golden brown and crispy. Using tongs, remove the cauliflower from the oil and place it on the prepared plate to absorb any excess oil. Repeat this process with the shrimp. Season both with a pinch of kosher salt. Remember to let the oil come back up to temperature in between batches. 6. Place the cauliflower and shrimp in a large serving bowl and top with corn, bruschetta mix, green onions, crumbled blue cheese, and Sriracha Mayo. Serve immediately.

Brunch

SERVES 4

½ cup + 1 Tbsp (140 mL) canola oil, divided

4 corn tortillas

Kosher salt

2 large ripe avocados

1 small red onion, finely diced

1 red bell pepper, finely diced

1 Roma tomato, finely diced

1 jalapeño pepper, seeded and diced

1 tsp (5 mL) chili powder

1 oz (30 g) tequila

1 tsp (5 mL) agave nectar

1 lb (450 g) large U.S. wild shrimp, peeled and deveined

4 sprigs cilantro, stems discarded

2 limes, quartered, for garnish

CABO CABO SHRIMP TOSTADAS

As you may have guessed from the recipe title, this was inspired by my fun and wild adventures in Cabo San Lucas, Mexico! I've only been there once but it was fantastic. If we ever meet, be sure to ask me about my Chad Kruger (yes, from Nickelback) and Jell-O shot story. In this dish, I chose to use sustainably sourced U.S. wild shrimp from the Gulf of Mexico, because their taste takes me back to the beautiful beaches, hot sun, and fresh flavors of Mexico. Grab a margarita and you'll be all set.

1. In a medium-size skillet, over medium-high heat, heat the ½ cup (125 mL) of canola oil to 350°F (180°C). Line a plate with paper towels. 2. Use tongs to place the corn tortillas, one at a time, in the hot oil and fry each side for approximately 1 minute, or until crispy and brown. Transfer the fried tortillas to the prepared plate and sprinkle with salt. Set aside. 3. Next, slice the avocados in half and remove the pits, but keep the flesh intact in the skin. Using a sharp knife, make four vertical cuts into each avocado half, not breaking the skin. Turn the avocado 90 degrees and make four more cuts for a criss-cross pattern. Using a tablespoon, carefully remove the diced avocado flesh from the skin and place it in a medium-size bowl. 4. Add the onions, bell peppers, tomatoes, jalapeño, and chili powder to the bowl with the avocados. Using the back of the spoon or a fork, mash the avocados in the bowl together with the other vegetables to make a guacamole, and set aside at room temperature until needed. 5. In a medium-size skillet, heat the remaining 1 Tbsp (15 mL) of canola oil over medium-high heat. Carefully add the tequila, agave nectar, and shrimp and cook for 1 to 2 minutes per side, or until the shrimp are cooked through and opaque in color. 6. Remove the shrimp from the skillet and place them in a clean bowl. Set aside at room temperature until needed. 7. On a clean work surface, lay out each tostada (fried corn tortilla). Spoon on the guacamole mixture and top with cooked shrimp and cilantro. Serve with a couple of lime quarters per person.

Quick & Easy

SERVES 4

2 Tbsp (30 mL) canola oil

2 cloves garlic, minced

1 1-inch (2.5 cm) piece fresh
ginger, minced

2 red Thai chilies, seeded and
diced

24 side strip shrimp, peeled
and deveined

Kosher salt and freshly ground
black pepper

8 leaves Bibb or iceberg
lettuce

Juice from 1–2 limes

NOTE: If you're buying the
side strip shrimp by weight,
you'll need approximately
2 lb (900 g).

CHILI LIME SIDE STRIPE SHRIMP LETTUCE WRAPS

Side stripe shrimp are light and sweet to taste and firm in texture. My favorite way to eat these babies is by dipping them into soy sauce. Sweet and salty, they're absolutely delicious!

1. In a large skillet, heat the canola oil over medium-high heat. Add the garlic, ginger, chilies, and shrimp. Season with salt and pepper to taste. Cook for 1 to 2 minutes per side, or until the shrimp have all turned opaque and are cooked through. 2. On a large, clean working surface, separate each lettuce leaf and lay flat. Next, divide the shrimp mixture among the leaves and squeeze some lime juice overtop. Now, wrap up the lettuce leaves and eat! Super fresh and super simple!

Party!

SERVES 4

4 medium sweet potatoes

¼ cup (60 mL) 2% milk

1 Tbsp (15 mL) harissa paste

½ tsp (2 mL) kosher salt

Freshly ground black pepper

1 Tbsp (15 mL) olive oil, plus more for drizzling

2 cloves garlic, minced

16 spot prawns, shells on

1 cup (250 mL) homemade or store-bought guacamole (see note)

Finishing salt (Maldon or Vancouver Island Sea Salt work well)

Zest from 1 lemon

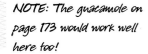

NOTE: The guacamole on page 173 would work well here too!

GARLIC SPOT PRAWN-STUFFED SWEET POTATOES

I may be biased because I live in Canada, but I must say that British Columbian spot prawns are the best in the world. Canadians didn't always have the luxury of eating these expensive prawns, though, because before 2006, most of the spot prawns harvested in Canada were exported to Asia. This recipe wasn't inspired by one of my Asian experiences, it was actually inspired by the time I spent living and working in Edinburgh, Scotland. I worked in a funky restaurant called Brecks, and we had a menu feature called Stuffed Jacket Potatoes. We had a great selection of delicious ingredients for fillings, but the bestseller was the one that used small cocktail shrimp. Can you imagine how well this luxurious potato would have sold with spot prawns in it? This recipe can easily be doubled for larger gatherings.

1. Preheat the oven to 400°F (200°C). Line a large baking tray with parchment paper. 2. Wash the sweet potatoes and pierce each one a few times with a fork. Place the potatoes on the prepared baking tray and bake for 40 to 50 minutes, or until soft. Remove the potatoes from the oven (leaving the oven switched on), and allow them to cool enough to handle comfortably. Slice the potatoes in half lengthwise and set aside at room temperature. 3. Turn down the oven to 375°F (190°C). 4. Using a spoon, scoop out the sweet potato flesh and place it in a medium-size bowl, leaving a thin layer of sweet potato flesh inside the skin. Be careful not to break the skins, as they'll be the bowls for the dish. Place the potato skins back on the baking tray. 5. Next, mash the sweet potato flesh with the milk, harissa paste, kosher salt, and pepper to taste. It should be chunky, not completely smooth. Set aside at room temperature. 6. In a skillet, heat the olive oil over low-medium heat. Add the garlic and cook for 1 to 2 minutes, or until soft and fragrant. Add the spot prawns and cook for 1 to 2 minutes per side, or until cooked through and opaque. 7. Fill each potato skin half with an equal amount of mashed sweet potato. Top each with 1 Tbsp (15 mL) of guacamole, two spot prawns, and some finishing salt. Finish the dish with a hit of lemon zest.

Lunch

SERVES 4

¼ cup (60 mL) canola oil

12 large U.S. wild shrimp, peeled and deveined

1 large pineapple, cut into chunks about ¾-inch (2 cm) thick

½ cup (125 mL) plain 0% Greek yogurt

1 Tbsp (15 mL) agave nectar

1 Tbsp (15 mL) ground allspice

1 tsp (5 mL) ground cinnamon

1 lime, cut into quarters

¼ cup (60 mL) crushed unsalted peanuts

2 sprigs cilantro, stems removed and leaves roughly chopped

Special equipment

8 metal or presoaked wooden skewers

GRILLED SHRIMP & PINEAPPLE SKEWERS

I love this recipe because it combines both sweetness and smokiness from the grill. I suggest keeping the shells on the shrimp when you're marinating or grilling them because it helps to lock the flavors in, and the shells are a huge source of flavor themselves. When I was kid, I used to work at a buffet restaurant, where I learned how to clean, prepare, and cook thousands of shrimp in a day. How many can you peel in a single minute? My record is 23!

1. Preheat the barbecue to 375°F (190°C). Dampen some paper towels with the canola oil and rub the grill grate so that no food sticks to it. 2. Place one shrimp on a skewer, followed by a piece of pineapple. Repeat until you have three pieces each of shrimp and pineapple on a skewer, then make up the remaining skewers. 3. Place the skewers on the grill and cook for 2 to 3 minutes per side. Remove them from the grill and wrap them in aluminum foil to keep warm. 4. In a small mixing bowl, combine the yogurt and agave nectar with the allspice and cinnamon. Mix well and then transfer to a small serving dish. 5. Serve the shrimp on a platter, garnished with lime quarters, crushed peanuts, and cilantro. Don't forget the dip!

Party!

VODKA SHRIMP TEMPURA

SERVES 6

1 large egg

½ cup (125 mL) cold vodka

½ cup (125 mL) cold soda
water

1 cup (250 mL) all-purpose
flour

½ cup (125 mL) cornstarch

12 large U.S. wild shrimp,
peeled and deveined

1 ½ cups (375 mL) canola oil

1 clove garlic, minced

½ cup (125 mL) light soy
sauce

Juice from 1 lime

Juice from 1 lemon

½ tsp (2 mL) fish sauce

½ tsp (2 mL) rice wine vinegar

Pinch of brown sugar

The secret to a great tempura is a light, airy, crispy batter. The cold vodka, which is made up of 60% water and 40% alcohol, cuts into the flour when mixed and reacts less intensely with the gluten in the flour than pure water would. At home, I tend to use Ketel One vodka. I suggest also using the vodka in my Matty's Famous Lobster Caesar (page 207) or a tasty Dutch mule to go alongside this shrimp recipe!

1. To make the tempura batter, combine the egg, vodka, and soda water in a large mixing bowl. Add the flour, and loosely mix together. Do not overstir the batter; it's okay if it has some lumps. Set aside at room temperature. **2.** Place the cornstarch in a medium-size mixing bowl. Dip each shrimp into the cornstarch to dust and gently shake off any excess cornstarch. Set aside at room temperature (the shrimp can sit out safely for 30 minutes). **3.** In a large, deep skillet or medium-size saucepan, heat the canola oil to 350°F (180°C). Line a plate with paper towels. **4.** Place a few shrimp at a time in the tempura batter to fully and evenly coat them, draining off any excess batter. **5.** Working in small batches, use tongs to carefully lower the shrimp into the hot oil and cook for 2 to 3 minutes, or until they are golden brown and float to the top of the oil. Using a metal slotted spoon, remove the shrimp from the oil and place them on the prepared plate to absorb any excess oil. Transfer the shrimp to a serving bowl. Remember to let the oil come back up to temperature in between batches. **6.** Meanwhile, in a small bowl, combine the garlic, soy sauce, lime juice, lemon juice, fish sauce, vinegar, and sugar. Mix well and serve as a dip for your crispy tempura shrimp.

Quick & Easy

SERVES 4

1 Tbsp (15 mL) canola oil

1 small white onion, finely chopped

2 cloves garlic, crushed (finely minced)

1 tsp (5 mL) yellow curry powder

1 tsp (5 mL) ground turmeric

1 tsp (5 mL) ground cumin

1 cup (250 mL) full-fat coconut milk

1 Tbsp (15 mL) soy sauce

Kosher salt and freshly ground black pepper

24 U.S. wild shrimp, peeled and deveined

2 cups (500 mL) freshly cooked white rice

1 lime, quartered

1 bunch Thai basil leaves

SHRIMP COCONUT CURRY

This rich coconut cream–based curry is a perfect dish for any cold winter night. There is something very comforting to the soul about a warm curry. If you're feeling a little under the weather, then this dish is for you. I use turmeric in this curry, as it is a natural anti-inflammatory and has been used for centuries as a home remedy.

1. In a large saucepan, heat the canola oil over medium-high heat. Add the onions, garlic, curry powder, turmeric, and cumin and sauté for 3 to 4 minutes, or until the onions are soft. Add ½ cup (125 mL) cold water, the coconut milk, and the soy sauce. Bring to a simmer and season to taste with salt and pepper. **2.** Turn down the heat to medium-low and then add the shrimp. Cook, stirring, for 3 to 4 minutes, or until the shrimp are bright pink and cooked through. **3.** Place the hot rice in a large serving dish or individual bowls and ladle the curry on top. Garnish with the lime quarters and Thai basil leaves.

SPOT PRAWN DUMPLINGS

SERVES 6

1 lb (450 g) spot prawns, peeled and finely diced

4 green onions, thinly chopped

1 egg white

1 Tbsp (15 mL) oyster sauce

1 Tbsp (15 mL) sesame oil

1 tsp (5 mL) low-sodium soy sauce, plus extra for dipping

1 cup (250 mL) chicken stock

1¼ cups (310 mL) wheat starch (see note)

¼ cup (60 mL) tapioca flour, plus extra for dusting

3 Tbsp (45 mL) cornstarch

1 tsp (5 mL) vegetable oil

NOTE: Wheat starch can be found at a specialty grocery store or online.

Going for dumplings is one of my favorite Saturday afternoon traditions. My fondest memory of an afternoon like this was going with my mom and grandmother Lelle to the legendary Bright Pearl in Toronto about 25 years ago. When I go out, I seem to always order far too much food, so I've learned to bring a bunch of friends with me on these excursions. Enjoy this dumpling recipe with many of your friends!

1. In a large mixing bowl, place the finely diced spot prawns, green onions, egg white, oyster sauce, sesame oil, and soy sauce. Gently mix and then place in the refrigerator for 1 hour, covered, to allow the flavors to combine. 2. In a small saucepan, bring the chicken stock to a boil over high heat. 3. Meanwhile, in a separate large mixing bowl, combine the wheat starch, tapioca flour, and cornstarch. Add the boiling chicken stock and the vegetable oil to these dry ingredients. Stir well to combine and make a dough. 4. Sprinkle a cutting board or clean surface with tapioca flour. While the dough is still warm, knead it using your hands until it becomes smooth. If it's too sticky, simply add more tapioca flour about 1 tsp (5 mL) at a time. 5. Cut the dough into four equal sections and roll each section into an 8-inch (20 cm) cylinder. Cut each cylinder into eight equal pieces. Keep the rest of the dough covered with a damp dish towel while you work. Using a rolling pin or the palm of your hand, gently roll out a piece of dough and press down to create a 2 ½- to 3-inch (6 to 8 cm) round. Place on a baking tray lined with parchment paper and set aside at room temperature. Repeat with the remaining dough pieces. 6. Using a teaspoon, evenly fill the middle of each round with the filling mixture. Fold over the top half of the dough to create a half circle. Ensure each dumpling is pressed down and sealed tight. Use the tines of a wet fork to press and close the edges. 7. Using a steamer on the stovetop, cook the dumplings over medium-high heat for 5 to 7 minutes, or until they're heated through and soft to the touch. Alternatively, in a medium-size or large saucepan, heat 1 Tbsp (15 mL) canola oil over medium-high heat, and cook the dumplings for 2 to 3 minutes per side, or until crisp and golden brown. 8. Serve the dumplings hot with soy sauce on the side for dipping.

Lunch

SERVES 6

24 large U.S. wild shrimp, peeled and deveined

3 Tbsp (45 mL) cornstarch

2 Tbsp (30 mL) sesame oil

2 cloves garlic, minced

2 green onions, thinly sliced

2 red Thai chilies, thinly sliced

½ cup (125 mL) full-fat mayonnaise

Juice from 1 lime

1 Tbsp (15 mL) Sriracha hot sauce

1 Tbsp (15 mL) toasted sesame seeds

Kosher salt and freshly ground black pepper

12 store-bought Chinese-style steamed buns (see note)

1 cup (250 mL) shredded purple cabbage

NOTE: Chinese-style steamed buns can be found in many Asian grocery stores.

STEAMED SHRIMP BUNS

My grandfather Mike recently passed away, and I miss him often. He was a serial entrepreneur and made both good and bad investments in his life. I always applauded him. After all, you never know what can happen unless you try. When I was young, I went to Vancouver to visit him for the first time and he took my mom, my sister, and me through Chinatown. I was in awe during our outing and the memory has stuck with me. These buns were inspired by my memories of that day.

1. In a medium-size mixing bowl, place the shrimp and cornstarch. Toss to coat all the shrimp and then set aside at room temperature. **2.** In a medium-size sauté pan or wok over high heat, sauté the sesame oil, garlic, green onions, and chilies for 1 to 2 minutes, until soft and fragrant. Add the shrimp and stir-fry for 2 to 3 minutes, or until all the shrimp are pink and cooked through. **3.** In a small mixing bowl, combine the mayonnaise, lime juice, Sriracha hot sauce, and sesame seeds. Season to taste with salt and pepper. Mix well. **4.** Heat the buns as per the package's instructions or to your desired liking. If the buns are whole, slice them in half as you would a hamburger bun. **5.** Spoon a dollop of Sriracha mayo on the bottom bun half. Top with shredded cabbage. Place two shrimp per bun on top of the cabbage, close the bun, and serve.

Brunch

SERVES 4

½ cup (125 mL) full-fat
   mayonnaise

2 Tbsp (30 mL) finely chopped
   flat-leaf parsley

1 tsp (5 mL) onion powder

1 tsp (5 mL) garlic powder

1 tsp (5 mL) cayenne pepper

1 tsp (5 mL) hot sauce

¼ cup (60 mL) diced English
   cucumber, skin on

¼ cup (60 mL) diced celery

1 Tbsp (15 mL) unsalted butter

1 lb (450 g) large U.S.
   wild shrimp, peeled and
   deveined

2 large avocados

¾ cup (175 mL) store-bought
   Hickory Sticks chips

STUFFED SHRIMP AVOCADOS

This recipe is the perfect snack on a warm summer's day! I would like to dedicate this dish to my good friend and ambassador of all things delicious and Mexican, Chef Andres Marquez. He has taught me so much about Mexican flavors and culture. *Salud, amigo!*

1. In a large mixing bowl, place the mayonnaise, parsley, onion powder, garlic powder, cayenne pepper, and hot sauce with the cucumbers and celery. Mix well, cover, and set aside in the refrigerator until needed. 2. In a medium-size skillet over medium-high heat, melt the butter. Add the shrimp and cook for 1 to 2 minutes per side, or until all the shrimp are pink and cooked through. Remove the shrimp from the skillet and allow them to cool at room temperature. Once cool, place them in a bowl, cover, and refrigerate until needed. 3. Just before serving, cut the avocados in half and carefully remove the pit, but leave the skins intact. Using a tablespoon, spoon out the avocado flesh and place it in a medium-size bowl. Mash the avocados and divide the flesh between the four avocado-skin bowls. 4. Add the shrimp to the parsley-cucumber mixture. 5. Place the stuffed avocados on a serving platter. Divide the shrimp mixture evenly on top of each. Top with the crispy Hickory Sticks chips and serve immediately.

TASTY
SIDES

BACON BRUSSELS SPROUTS

SERVES 2–4

1 lb (450 g) fresh Brussels sprouts, outer leaves removed, sprouts cut in half lengthwise

2 Tbsp (30 mL) extra-virgin olive oil

Kosher salt

4 slices thick-cut bacon, cooked and crumbled

¼ cup (60 mL) grated Parmigiano-Reggiano cheese

½ lemon (cut lengthwise)

If you want this dish to knock the socks off your guests, cook the Brussels sprouts in the bacon fat after you've crisped up the bacon.

1. Prepare an ice bath. 2. In a large saucepan, bring 8 cups (2 L) of cold water to a boil over high heat. Blanch the sprouts for 2 to 3 minutes, or until they turn bright green. Drain the sprouts and immediately shock them in the ice bath. This will help to minimize the bitterness. 3. Place the Brussels sprouts in a hot skillet over medium heat. Drizzle the olive oil over them. Cook, stirring occasionally so they don't burn, for 6 to 8 minutes, or until the sprouts are soft, slightly golden brown, and starting to crisp. Add a pinch of salt, stir well, and remove from the heat. 4. Arrange the Brussels sprouts on a serving platter and garnish with the bacon and cheese. 5. In the same hot skillet, grill the lemon half, flesh side down, for to 2 minutes, or until marked and slightly caramelized. Squeeze the lemon juice over the hot sprouts just before serving.

THE 1979 BLUE CHEESE WEDGE SALAD

SERVES 4

1 cup (250 mL) cherry tomato halves

4 slices thick-cut strip bacon, cooked crisp and crumbled

Juice from 1 lemon

½ cup (125 mL) full-fat sour cream

¼ cup (60 mL) 2% milk

¼ cup (60 mL) crumbled blue cheese

Freshly ground black pepper

1 large head iceberg lettuce, quartered

1 tsp (5 mL) za'atar seasoning

¼ cup (60 mL) chopped chives

I was born in 1979, when this classic salad ruled all dinner tables. Let's take it back retro-style and enjoy this timeless classic. Real classics always make a comeback!

1. In a medium-size mixing bowl, place the tomatoes, crumbled bacon, and lemon juice. Toss to combine and then set aside at room temperature. 2. In a separate mixing bowl, place the sour cream, milk, blue cheese, and pepper to taste. Whisk together until you have a smooth dressing. Add more milk if it's too thick. 3. On each of four side plates, lay a lettuce quarter. Top with the tomato mixture and drizzle with the dressing. Sprinkle with za'atar seasoning and finish with the chopped chives.

MATTY'S BBQ'D MEXICAN STREET CORN

SERVES 4

2 Tbsp (30 mL) nonfat plain yogurt

1 tsp (5 mL) ground cumin

1 tsp (5 mL) dried oregano

1 tsp (5 mL) chili powder

4 ears of corn, husked

½ cup (125 mL) salted butter, softened

½ cup (125 mL) crumbled Cotija or feta cheese, for garnish

2 limes, quartered, for garnish

Mexican street corn is known as *elote* in Spanish. This side dish is the quintessential example of perfect street food! When you walk the streets of most Mexican cities and towns you'll see vendors selling this style of corn. I love to kick up the heat on mine and to add lots of Cotija cheese. Don't forget to have fresh limes on hand for some added acidity.

1. Preheat the barbecue to 375°F (190°C). 2. In a medium-size mixing bowl, combine the yogurt, cumin, oregano, and chili powder. Set aside at room temperature. 3. Grill the corn ears, turning occasionally, for 6 to 8 minutes, or until slightly charred with grill marks. Remove from the grill. 4. Dip or brush soft butter onto each piece of corn and then brush on the yogurt-spice mixture. Garnish with the cheese and serve with a couple of quarters of lime on the side.

QUICK & EASY NO-KNEAD BEER BREAD

MAKES 1 8 ½- X 4 ½-INCH (20 X 11 CM) LOAF

1 ¼ tsp (6 mL) dry active yeast

4 ½ cups (1.1 L) all-purpose flour, divided, plus more for dusting

1 bottle (355 mL) beer (your favorite kind although I suggest an ale)

1 ½ tsp (7 mL) fine salt

Cornmeal, for dusting

If you've ever made fresh bread at home, you'll know it can take quite some time—so you'll thank me for this recipe! This bread not only has incredible flavor and texture, it's also simple to make.

1. In a large bowl, whisk together the yeast, ½ cup (125 mL) of the flour, and ½ cup (125 mL) warm water. Cover and allow to sit in a warm spot for about 30 minutes. 2. Using a wooden spoon, stir the remaining flour, the beer, and salt into the bowl of batter. Mix well with your hands until all the flour has been absorbed and you have a thick, sticky dough. Be careful not to overmix. Cover loosely with a clean dish towel and let rise in a warm, draft-free spot for 2 hours, or until doubled in size. To remove the dough from the mixing bowl, lightly spray the edges of the bread with nonstick cooking spray. 3. Place the dough on a well-floured surface. Generously flour the top of the dough and shape it with your hands to form a loaf. 4. Dust a baking tray with cornmeal. 5. Transfer the dough loaf to the baking tray and sprinkle the top with more flour. Cover loosely with the dish towel and it let rise for 30 to 40 minutes in a warm, draft-free spot. 6. Preheat the oven to 425°F (220°C). Place a small ovenproof dish of warm water on a lower rack to humidify the oven and prevent the bread from cracking. 7. Place the baking tray with the loaf on the rack above the pan of water in the oven. Bake for 35 to 40 minutes, or until the loaf is golden brown. 8. Allow the bread to cool completely on a wire rack before slicing and serving.

 NOTE: Time is your friend with this recipe. Don't rush and make sure you allow the dough to fully rise.

ROASTED BEET & AGAVE CAPRESE SALAD

SERVES 2

2–3 large red beets

1 container (18 oz/500 g) bocconcini cheese

4 basil leaves, stems discarded

2 Tbsp (30 mL) extra-virgin olive oil

¼ cup (60 mL) pine nuts, toasted and chopped

2 Tbsp (30 mL) agave nectar

Kosher salt and freshly ground black pepper

This was one of the first side salads I made for the menu at Rock Lobster on Ossington Avenue (our first restaurant) back in 2011. Beets and agave are a match made in heaven. If you ever see a brand of agave nectar called Sheer, grab it! It's amazing, and it's owned by a good friend of mine, Eric Brass.

1. Preheat the oven to 375°F (190°C). 2. Wash and scrub each beet under cold water. Wrap each beet individually in aluminum foil and place in the oven. Cook for approximately 1 ½ hours, or until you can poke them easily with a fork or knife. Remove the beets from the oven and allow them to cool at room temperature until cool enough to handle. 3. Using plastic or latex disposable gloves, gently peel the beets' skin off with your fingers and thumbs. The skins should peel back very easily. Cut the beets into ¼-inch-thick (6 mm) wheels (approximately four slices per beet) and then set aside at room temperature. 4. Slice the bocconcini cheese into ¼-inch-thick (6 mm) wheels. 5. Chiffonade the basil leaves by stacking them, rolling them tight, and thinly slicing them perpendicular to the roll. 6. On each serving plate, lay one beet wheel and then one cheese wheel on top, and continue to alternate them. Drizzle with the olive oil and garnish with the pine nuts, agave nectar, basil chiffonade, and salt and pepper to taste.

STUFF YOUR OWN POTATOES

SERVES 2–4

2 large Yukon Gold potatoes, washed and cleaned

1 Tbsp (15 mL) canola oil

Kosher salt and freshly ground black pepper

1 cup (250 mL) medium-ground chicken

½ cup (125 mL) crumbled blue cheese

4 slices bacon, cooked and crumbled

½ cup (125 mL) full-fat sour cream

Drizzle of hot sauce

4–6 fresh chives, finely chopped

Exactly like the recipe name says, you're going to stuff your own potatoes here. If you're not feeling my stuffing choices, simply choose what you like and stuff away!

1. Preheat the oven to 425°F (220°C). 2. Using a fork, prick the potatoes all over, 5 to 10 times each. Drizzle with the canola oil and season with salt. Wrap each potato individually in aluminum foil, set on a baking tray, and bake for 45 minutes to 1 hour, or until a fork slides in easily. 3. In the meantime, heat a large skillet over medium heat. Add the ground chicken and cook, stirring occasionally and breaking up the meat, for 6 to 8 minutes, or until slightly brown. Sprinkle with salt and pepper to taste. Mix well, allow to cool, and set aside at room temperature. 4. Once the potatoes have finished cooking, slice each one lengthwise from end to end, without cutting them in half. Using your hands, pop open the potatoes by gently squeezing the bottom and pushing upward to create a pocket. The potato flesh will stay inside the potato. 5. Divide the ground chicken evenly between each potato pocket. Return the potatoes to the baking tray and put them back in the warm oven for about 5 minutes so that the chicken comes back up to temperature. Remove from the oven, and garnish with the blue cheese, crumbled bacon, a small dollop of sour cream, a drizzle of hot sauce, and chives.

COCKTAILS

HOT APPLE CIDER BRÛLÉE

SERVES 1

1 cup (250 mL) dry hard
   apple cider

1 oz (30 mL) whiskey

1 Tbsp (15 mL) honey

1 Empire or McIntosh apple

1 tsp (5 mL) granulated sugar

1 long sprig fresh thyme,
   picked

Special equipment

Kitchen torch

When I make this drink, I use Brickworks Cider. It's not only my personal favorite, it's also made in my home city of Toronto—and created by one of my good buddies, Chris Noll. Thanks to Nollzy, Adam, Sugsy, and the rest of the team for crafting such a great product.

1. In a small saucepan, heat the apple cider, whiskey, and honey over medium heat for 3 to 5 minutes, or until the liquid simmers. Turn down the heat to low to keep the ingredients warm. 2. Place the apple on a clean work surface and, using a sharp knife, cut it vertically to the right of the core to make an apple half. Eat the left side of the apple. (Tip: An apple a day keeps the doctor away!) Standing that apple half up, vertically cut a long wheel piece, about ¾-inch (2 cm) thick. Eat the remaining apple. 3. Transfer the hot cider to a large mug wide enough to hold the apple wheel comfortably, being careful not to splash. 4. To garnish, lay the apple wheel flat on a plate, sprinkle the sugar on top, and, using the kitchen torch, slowly caramelize the sugar. 5. Add the thyme to the glass and top with the apple wheel. 6. Grab a good book and a warm blanket, and get comfy with this cold-weather cocktail.

MATTY'S FAMILY FESTIVE EGGNOG WITH A TWIST

SERVES 1

1 cup (250 mL) eggnog

1 oz (30 mL) vodka

1 cup (250 mL) chocolate ice cream

1 of your favorite chocolate cookies, crumbled

Whipped cream, for garnish

Grated fresh nutmeg, for garnish

NOTE: Remove the vodka for a nonalcoholic drink.

If it's Christmas in my house, this eggnog is in some of my family members' hands! 'Tis the season to be merry. Since the holidays can be quite crazy, you may need a few of these.

1. In a tall glass, place the eggnog and vodka. Mix well. 2. Add the ice cream, and then garnish with the cookie crumbs, whipped cream (as much as you like), and grated fresh nutmeg.

MATTY'S FAMOUS LOBSTER CAESAR

SERVES 1

1 lime quarter

Montreal steak spice, to rim

1 cup (250 mL) ice cubes

½–¾ cup (125–175 mL) Clamato juice

1½ oz (45 mL) vodka

2 dashes of hot sauce

2 dashes of Worcestershire sauce

Freshly ground black pepper

1 stalk celery

1 lemon quarter

½ piece cooked lobster tail, shell on (3–4 oz/90–120 g)

Special equipment

1 wooden skewer

This award-winning cocktail has been written about by several media outlets, including my American friends at *USA Today*, since 2011 when I created it! I could not be more thankful. It was a staple beverage at our Rock Lobster Food Co. restaurants. What makes this Caesar better than the others, you ask? Well, I would have to say it's the fresh ingredients I use and the huge lobster tail I add for garnish!

1. Moisten the rim of a beer stein with a lime wedge and then rim it with the steak spice. 2. Fill the glass with the ice. Pour in the Clamato juice and vodka, and then add the hot sauce, Worcestershire sauce, and pepper. Give it all a gentle stir. 3. To garnish, insert the celery stalk and perch the lemon quarter on the glass rim. 4. Skewer the lobster tail using a wooden skewer and then pop it into the glass beside the celery. Enjoy!

NOTE: Swap out the Clamato juice for tomato juice and you'll get a Bloody Mary (you're welcome, my American friends).

MEXICAN BLOODY MARY

SERVES 1

2 medium Roma tomatoes, seeded and diced, or 1 cup (250 mL) canned tomato juice

1 ½ oz (45 mL) vodka

1 tsp (5 mL) Worcestershire sauce

1 tsp (5 mL) lemon juice

1 tsp (5 mL) finely chopped cilantro leaves

1 tsp (5 mL) fresh oregano leaves

1 dash of hot sauce

2 cups (500 mL) ice cubes, divided

Kosher salt and freshly ground black pepper

1 lime wedge

This drink can be used as a chaser after sipping a nice tequila, or try adding a bottle of beer to make a Mexican *michelada*! The key to a Bloody Mary is to stir it well in a shaker with ice. If you shake it, the drink will become too frothy. I like to use Ketel One vodka in this.

1. If using fresh tomatoes, juice them with a juicer. 2. In a cocktail shaker, combine the tomatoes with the vodka, Worcestershire sauce, lemon juice, cilantro, oregano, and hot sauce. Add 1 cup (250 mL) ice to the shaker. Gently stir to combine, but do not shake. 3. To assemble the drink, fill a glass with the remaining unused ice and strain the drink over it. Garnish with the lime wedge.

"BIG KIDS'" SALTED CARAMEL VANILLA VODKA FLOAT

1 cup (250 mL) vanilla ice cream

¾ cup (175 mL) cola

¼ cup (60 mL) 2% milk

1 oz (30 mL) vodka

1 Tbsp (15 mL) caramel sauce

1 Tbsp (15 mL) crumbled Candied Bacon (page 224)

Himalayan sea salt

I used to love floats as a kid. Root beer and vanilla ice cream, say what! Floats are now back in style, so I thought it was time to make one for the "big kids." Try kicking this recipe up a notch by adding a dark spirit like Crown Royal. I like to use Ketel One vodka in this.

1. In a large parfait or pint glass, place the ice cream. In a small bowl, combine the cola, milk, and vodka. Pour this over the ice cream. Drizzle with caramel sauce and garnish with crumbled candied bacon and a very small pinch of Himalayan sea salt. 2. Serve with a large spoon.

KYOTO GREEN TEA MOJITO

1 yuzu fruit, quartered and
divided (find this at a
specialty produce market)

1 Tbsp (15 mL) agave nectar

4 mint leaves

1 cup (250 mL) crushed ice

1 cup (250 mL) cold green tea

2 oz (60 mL) Futsū-shu sake
(standard sake)

1 Fuji apple wheel, for garnish
(see page 203)

I recently had the opportunity to visit Kyoto, Japan, and it was a real pleasure. The city is rich in history and tradition in part because it's home to thousands of temples. It's also the birthplace of *kaiseki*, a traditional multicourse dining experience with 20+ small, perfect plates. It's not an inexpensive experience, but I thought it was definitely worth every penny! With great dining comes great drink pairings, and it was in Kyoto that I really fell in love with sake and became inspired to create this recipe.

1. In a tall, wide glass, place two yuzu fruit quarters, the agave nectar, and two mint leaves. Using a muddler, grind the ingredients together to combine all the flavors. 2. Add the ice and then the green tea and sake. Gently stir. 3. Garnish with two mint leaves, two yuzu quarters, and the apple wheel.

PETTIT'S PIMM'S CUP

SERVES 1

1 cup (250 mL) ice cubes

4 slices cucumber, divided

2 slices orange (wheel), divided

2 slices lemon (wheel), divided

4 strawberries, sliced in half lengthwise, divided

2 oz (60 mL) Pimm's No. 1 liqueur

¾ cup (175 mL) soda water

1 small sprig mint, for garnish

Picture this: it's a hot summer day, birds are chirping, you're sitting at a backyard barbecue party, and you see a pitcher of this tasty drink come toward you. Yes, I thought you'd smile! Pimm's has been around for nearly 200 years and was invented in the U.K. I prefer to use soda water in this recipe because it has fewer calories than the traditionally used ginger ale, but use whichever one you prefer.

1. Fill a tall glass close to the top with the ice. Add three cucumber slices, one orange slice, one lemon slice, and six strawberry halves. Pour in the Pimm's and then the soda water. 2. Garnish with the remaining fruit and a mint sprig. Tastes like summer in a glass!

SUMMER SANGRIA PARTY PITCHER

SERVES 4–6

4 cups (1 L) ice cubes

½ cup (125 mL) blueberries

½ cup (125 mL) sliced peaches, cut into thin wheels

1 lemon, cut into thin wheels

1 lime, cut into thin wheels

1 bottle (750 mL) your choice of white wine

1 can (355 mL) soda water

1 cup (250 mL) cranberry juice

2 Tbsp (30 mL) agave nectar

NOTE: If you want to make this a red sangria, feel free to use a merlot or zinfandel. These are generally fruit-forward too.

I fell in love with sangria on the beaches of southern Spain. I usually make this white sangria in August when the summer heat is at its peak and delicious local (Ontario) peaches are in season. Using a sauvignon blanc or pinot grigio makes for a light, crisp, and very fruit-forward sangria. Make sure the wine is very cold.

1. Fill a large pitcher halfway with ice. Add the blueberries, peaches, lemon, and lime. Add the wine, soda water, cranberry juice, and agave nectar. Stir well. Top the pitcher with any remaining ice. 2. Serve the sangria in small cocktail glasses with more ice.

THE CLUB MED CAESAR

SERVES 1

Lime wedge

Celery salt, to rim

Ground fresh basil, to rim

1 cup (250 mL) ice cubes

1½ oz (45 mL) vodka

2 dashes of balsamic vinegar

½–¾ cup (125–175 mL)
   Clamato juice

1 sprig fresh rosemary, for
   garnish

1 sprig fresh basil, for garnish

Sometimes people say to me that Caesars are too thick or have too much seafood flavor. If you find yourself feeling that way, try this version. The balsamic vinegar adds just enough acidity to cut through the Clamato juice, and the fresh rosemary helps balance the entire drink. I like to use Ketel One vodka in this.

1. Moisten the rim of a pint glass using the lime wedge and then rim it with celery salt and ground fresh basil. 2. Place the ice in the glass and then add the vodka, balsamic vinegar, and Clamato juice. Stir well. Garnish with the rosemary and basil sprigs. Enjoy every drop!

THE McCLURE BLOODY MARY

SERVES 1

1 cup (250 mL) ice

1 oz (30 mL) vodka

½ cup (125 mL) tomato juice

Juice from 1 lemon

1 tsp (5 mL) freshly grated or
jarred horseradish

3 dashes of Sriracha hot sauce

2 dashes of Worcestershire
sauce

1–2 cherry tomatoes, for
garnish

1–2 stuffed olives (your favorite
kind), for garnish

1–2 baby carrots, for garnish

1 cocktail onion, for garnish

Pickle spear, for garnish

Special equipment

1 cocktail skewer

This drink is inspired by a very good friend of mine, Joe McClure, whose epony-mous company is based in Detroit, Michigan. McClures started in the late 2000s with a selection of homemade pickles and has now grown into a massive brand. Joe and I have worked on several cool events and projects together. Stay tuned for what we have coming next.

1. Fill a pint glass with ice. Add the vodka, tomato juice, lemon juice, horseradish, hot sauce, and Worcestershire sauce. Gently stir to combine the flavors. 2. Thread the cherry tomatoes, olives, baby carrots, and a cocktail onion onto the cocktail skewer. Garnish your drink with the cocktail skewer and the pickle spear.

TOES IN THE SAND ISLAND RUM PUNCH

SERVES 4–6

½ cup (125 mL) granulated sugar

4 cups (1 L) ice cubes, plus extra

8 oz (240 mL) dark rum

1 cup (250 mL) pineapple juice

1 cup (250 mL) coconut water

2 sprigs fresh thyme

Grated fresh nutmeg, for garnish

2 limes, quartered, for garnish

This recipe is named after the lyrics of one of my favorite Zac Brown Band songs. It's a song that instantly transports me to vacation mode. The combo of dark rum and fruit in this drink gives it a well-balanced sweetness.

1. Make a simple syrup by adding the sugar to ½ cup (125 mL) cold water in a small saucepan over medium-high heat. Cook, stirring, until the sugar crystals have completely dissolved. Remove from the heat and allow the syrup to cool completely. Place ¼ cup (60 mL) aside for this recipe, and store the rest in an airtight container in the refrigerator for up to 1 month. 2. Fill a large pitcher with ice. Add the rum and the reserved simple syrup. Stir to mix well. Add the pineapple juice, coconut water, and thyme. Mix to combine the flavors. 3. Set out four to six small rocks glasses and fill each one with ice. Pour the rum punch into the glasses. Garnish each one with a sprinkle of fresh nutmeg on top and a lime wedge. Welcome to vacation mode!

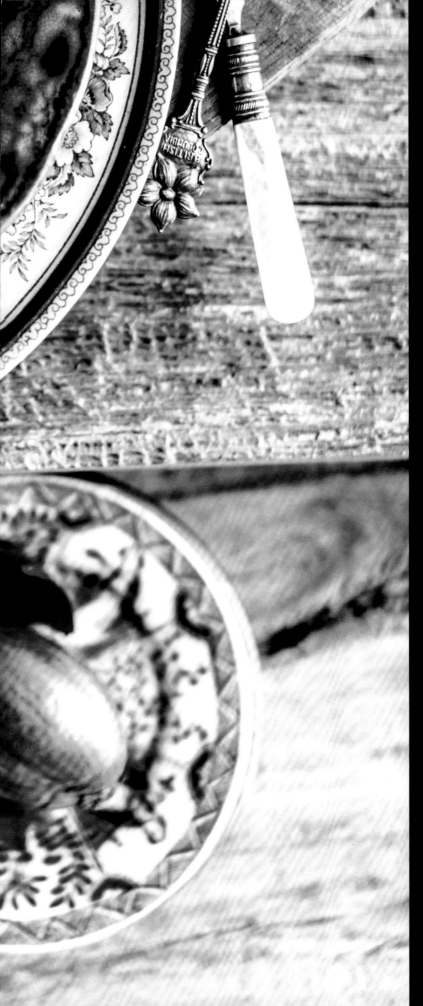

SAUCES & STAPLES

CANDIED BACON

MAKES 8–12 PIECES

1 lb (450 g) smoked bacon

Drizzle of canola oil

¼ cup (60 mL) maple syrup

2 Tbsp (30 mL) chili flakes

This is the perfect garnish for desserts, cocktails, salads, soups, and practically any appetizer that needs a crunchy sweet note!

1. Preheat the oven to 400°F (200°C). Line a baking tray with parchment paper. 2. On the prepared baking tray, lay out the bacon in long and flat strips, making sure not to overlap the pieces. Evenly drizzle some canola oil across the strips and then pour the maple syrup overtop. 3. Bake the bacon for 10 to 12 minutes, and then flip the pieces over and bake for another 3 to 5 minutes, or until crispy. Remove the bacon from the oven and sprinkle with chili flakes while it's hot. 4. Once the bacon pieces have cooled, use them immediately or transfer to an airtight container and store in the refrigerator for up to 1 week.

CLARIFIED BUTTER

MAKES ¾ CUP (175 ML)

1 cup (250 mL) salted butter

If you can make clarified butter rather than simple melted butter, do so! It's easy. This clean butter liquid is full of healthy fat and you can heat, cool, and solidify it several times.

1. In a small saucepan, melt the butter over medium heat. When it starts to froth, remove the pan from the heat and do not stir the butter. 2. Using a small fine-mesh strainer set over a bowl, slowly pour the melted butter through the strainer into the bowl to remove the frothy solid fats. 3. Transfer the clarified butter to an airtight container and refrigerate overnight, until it has fully hardened. 4. When needed, melt the butter in a saucepan and dip your favorite seafood in it or pan-fry your vegetables in it. 5. This will keep refrigerated for up to 2 weeks.

LEMON CAPER DIP

MAKES ¾ CUP (175 ML)

½ cup (125 mL) full-fat
  mayonnaise

2 Tbsp (30 mL) finely chopped
  capers

Juice from 1 lemon

¼ cup (60 mL) finely chopped
  flat-leaf parsley

1 tsp (2 mL) mustard powder

Kosher salt and freshly ground
  black pepper

When I was a child, my dad used to make us his classic dip, which consisted of sour cream and dry French onion soup mix. This may sound odd, but eating it with salty plain potato chips made it a complete winner, especially when you're 8 years old. Thanks for teaching me how to cook, Dad (wink wink). Try this adult version for your next chip and dip party!

1. In a medium-size bowl, place all the ingredients. Mix well. 2. Transfer the dip to an airtight container and store in the refrigerator for up to 1 week.

MATTY'S SEAFOOD COCKTAIL SAUCE

MAKES ¾ CUP (175 ML)

½ cup (125 mL) ketchup

¼ cup (60 mL) prepared white
  horseradish, strained

Juice from 1 lemon

1 tsp (5 mL) white vinegar

4 dashes of Worcestershire
  sauce

Kosher salt and freshly ground
  black pepper

4 dashes of hot sauce

I've been making this recipe for years. I make it almost every other day because it's the perfect sauce or dip for any hot or chilled shellfish. If you want to try something fun, add a bit of bourbon or rye whiskey for extra zing!

1. In a small bowl, place the ketchup, horseradish, lemon juice, vinegar, Worcestershire sauce, salt, and pepper, and stir well. Slowly add the hot sauce, dash by dash, and taste as you go, so you don't make it too hot. 2. Transfer the sauce to an airtight container and store in the refrigerator for up to 1 month.

PONZU SAUCE

MAKES ¾ CUP (175 ML)

½ cup (125 mL) soy sauce

Juice from 2 lemons

Juice from 1 lime

1 Tbsp (15 mL) rice wine
vinegar

1 tsp (5 mL) grated fresh ginger

I fell in love with ponzu sauce when I was in Japan, where it was served with sushi and sashimi. It combines salty and savory with light and citrus-like flavors, and is one of my favorite elements of Japanese cuisine.

1. In a medium-size bowl, whisk all the ingredients together until fully combined.
2. Transfer the sauce to an airtight container and store in the refrigerator for up to 1 week.

SRIRACHA MAYO

MAKES 1 CUP (250 ML)

1 cup (250 mL) full-fat
mayonnaise

2 Tbsp (30 mL) Sriracha hot
sauce

Juice from 1 lemon

1 tsp (5 mL) rice wine vinegar

Kosher salt and freshly ground
black pepper

Sriracha hot sauce may be one of the most popular food trends ever. It's in or on almost everything these days!

1. In a large bowl, whisk the mayonnaise, Sriracha, lemon juice, and vinegar until fully combined. Season to taste with salt and pepper. 2. Transfer the mayo to an airtight container and store in the refrigerator for up to 1 week.

ACKNOWLEDGMENTS

Thanks!

As I wrote this, I was singing and listening to The Beatles. How very appropriate for this section of this book . . . "all you need is love!"

I can't thank my mom, dad, and sister enough for taking the time and care and providing the unconditional love and understanding that helped me grow into the person I am today. I remember when I was just a kid and I used to have a ton of energy and I was a handful to deal with . . . Okay, so not too much has changed. To help burn that energy, they would keep me busy by enrolling me in every activity, summer camp, and sport possible, even when most of the time we didn't have the extra money to do so. My mom and dad always worked so hard to give my sister, Amie, and me everything we needed, and most of the time everything we wanted. Looking back now as an adult, I know it's easy and clichéd to say but I really do have the

Momma: You constantly put others' needs before your own, without wanting anything in return. I remember when I was a kid, and you and Dad used to welcome and help many young teens who sometimes just needed a small lift and family love . . . Who does that? You do! You're the best, momma. Thank you, and remember I will always be your little smiling boy!

Dad: You're my best friend, in-house graphic design team, and number one supporter. Thank you, thank you, thank you. Just like Mom, you've always put my feelings and needs before your own. Do you remember when you were my baseball coach because no other parent would do it? You stepped up again as you always do. Everyone reading this book should know that just like in my first book, my dad did all the hand-drawn shellfish art! It's so cool how you've contributed to these

Amiers: My associate in-family editor, I can't thank you enough for always caring so much for me and supporting whatever I have going on in my life. Do you remember teaching me how to read and write? I do! It seems like only yesterday that we were watching *E.T.* together and then you'd read the *E.T.* book to me. Here's to a lot of smiles and laughs in the future for us.

Dana, my sweet: You are constantly the voice of reason and I know I've said that before but we all know it's so true. When people say yes or that's a good idea, you say, "Wait, maybe, did you think about this first?" This is one of the many reasons why you help complete me. I love you. It takes two to tango, so thank you for being my dancing partner! Xoxo

Thank you to my publisher, Robert McCullough; my editor, Zoe Maslow; my designer, Terri Nimmo; PRHC Prez Kristin Cochrane; and the entire Appetite by Random House team: I consider you guys my family. It's been a fun, crazy 6 years since we first met at Rock Lobster on Ossington, and since that day, you've all treated me with such kindness. I didn't know if the day would come that I would be asked to work with you on another book, but it came, and I appreciate the confidence you have in me! Thank you so much.

Caiti McLelland: Cheers to you. You take my chicken-scratch recipes, notes, and stories, and transform them into wonderful words that truly reflect my personality.

Ksenija Hotic: I'm honored to have worked with you on your first cookbook. Your photographs and food styling have made this book immeasurably better, and I am so grateful for your hard work and talent. I'm excited to see what you do next!

To my amazing representation and PR team—Roseanna Plutino, Cathy LeDrew, Jordie McTavish, Sean Beckingham, and Marian Staresinic: you guys all rock. You have so much trust and faith in me, thank you for that. I always look forward to our discussions on how to tackle to the next opportunity or even tough challenges ahead. Your guidance, knowledge, and positive outlook help make my job very easy.

Last but certainly not least, to my friends, fans, and everyone and anyone who has supported me since Day One: none of this would be possible without you. The books, TV shows, restaurants, retail brand, nothing. I owe it all to the love and support you guys have always shown me. Here's to the next chapter.

Much love,
MDP

INDEX

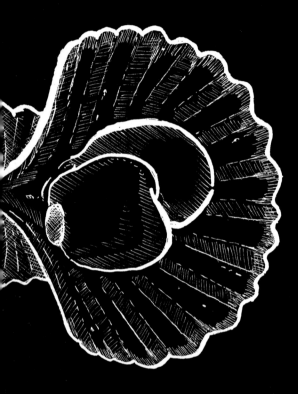